The Cambridge

GHOST BOOK

This book is dedicated to

RICHARD CHARLES HALLIDAY
(1957–1997)

Brother and Friend

The Cambridge
GHOST BOOK

by

Robert Halliday & Alan Murdie

Fern House

An original paperback first published in 2000 by
Fern House, High Street, Haddenham,
ELY, Cambridgeshire CB6 3XA

A catalogue record for this book
is available from the British Library

ISBN 1 902702 07 7

Jacket design by Matthew Pettitt
Printed in England by TJ International Ltd, Padstow

CONTENTS

THE AUTHORS

ROBERT HALLIDAY was born in Cambridge. He holds a BA degree in history from North London Polytechnic and an MA degree in history from State University of New York at Binghamton, USA. He has worked as an archaeologist and museum assistant and has lectured and published articles on history, archaeology and folklore.

ALAN MURDIE LLB, Barrister, was born near Bury St Edmunds. He is Chairman of the Ghost Club, the world's oldest psychical research organisation, founded in Cambridge in the Victorian era. He is also a council member of the Society of Psychical Research and has written and broadcast extensively on paranormal topics. He has conducted many investigations into ghosts and poltergeist phenomena both in the UK and abroad.

Introduction

Cambridge, England, has been the setting for a wide variety of supernatural phenomena, and can claim to be one of the most haunted locations in the British Isles. Its history – and even its geographical setting – have made it an important centre for the observation of paranormal activity.

A settlement was established in Roman times at the southern edge of the Fens, an area of marshes and swamps which was not properly drained until the seventeenth century. As its name suggests, Cambridge originated as a crossing point on the River Cam, which flows into the River Ouse and then to the Wash.

Cambridge thus stood at the northernmost point where travellers could avoid the Fen marshes. It developed into a centre of communications and a trading point for boats from the Fen waterways, becoming the county town of Cambridgeshire in the tenth century.

It is now generally agreed that groups of scholars wishing to pursue higher education first came to Cambridge in 1209; University education has continued without interruption ever since.

Much of the distinctive character of Cambridge is derived from the University buildings, in particular the colleges. Peterhouse, the oldest of these, was founded in 1284, as a place where university students and staff could live and study, while Robinson College was opened as recently as 1974.

Officially created a city in 1955, Cambridge is now a commercial and administrative centre, and a thriving tourist resort, with a University of international importance.

Ghosts and hauntings have been observed in Cambridge for centuries. The city is packed with historic buildings. A rich variety of eccentric and unusual people have lived in those buildings, and their activities may have left a lasting impression on the historic fabric.

Some Cambridge students have been sufficiently interested in psychic phenomena to record and analyse their own experiences of the supernatural, and study the experiences of others. In the nineteenth century, members of the University formed the Ghost Club and the Society for Psychical Research. Partly because of this, the archives of the Society for Psychical Research, one of the largest collections of paranormal studies in the world, were deposited in the University Library in 1991.

T C Lethbridge (*see* T rinity College), a paranormal investigator who lived and worked in Cambridge, was the first person to suggest that ghosts often appear in damp areas, and that supernatural discharges might therefore be conducted through water vapour. This led him to reason that the location of Cambridge – on a river near the Fen marshes – might make it a fertile breeding ground for ghosts.

Scholars such as M R James and Arthur Gray have drawn on their knowledge of University life and traditions to write ghost stories which have further developed the city's supernatural heritage.

The authors inaugurated the Cambridge Ghost Walk in 1998. It has attracted great interest from residents, tourists and students alike. Some people coming on the walk have told us about their own experiences, which have been often proved fascinating.

This book recounts some of the ghost stories associated with Cambridge. We have as far as possible investigated and authenticated each story, and we hope that all our readers will find something here to hold their interest.

THE ABBEY HOUSE

If any building deserves the title of the most haunted house in Cambridge it may be the Abbey House.

The Abbey House is named after Barnwell Priory, a monastery which stood on the site between 1112 and 1539. (A priory was a monastery run by a prior, an official of a slightly lower rank than an abbot, but Barnwell Priory came to be remembered as an Abbey with the passage of time.) Most of the Priory was demolished after its closure in 1539, and the Abbey House may have been built with material from the Priory ruins.

The House stands in a modern street near Newmarket Road,

on the east of Cambridge, obscured by trees and a high, crumbling wall. The rooftops of the old house peer strangely over the Victorian terraces and the modern buildings which now engulf the area. By the nineteenth century it was widely believed that the Abbey House was haunted, and ghosts were said to roam the building and its grounds.

Jacob Butler, a former owner of the house, is believed to be one of the ghosts whose spirit remains connected with the building. Educated at Christ's College between 1698 and 1703, he was a towering, burly giant of a man, standing six feet four inches tall. He became a lawyer, and often involved himself in

Jacob Butler

legal disputes to reform corrupt practices in Cambridge.

Inheriting the Abbey House in 1714, he enlarged it, giving it the appearance it presents today. When fairs were held at Cambridge, Jacob Butler would hold a banquet at the house for the giants, dwarfs and other performers.

In his old age, when he took pride in being Britain's oldest practising barrister, Jacob Butler set up his coffin in the Abbey House, inviting visitors to sit in it and drink wine with him.

One of his favourite companions of his last years was a dog, who he trained to walk on its hind legs. This died in 1765, and his unhappiness at the death of his pet hastened his death, later that year, at the age of 84.

A large and eccentric procession followed his funeral; his

body was carried to the nearby church of St Andrew the Less on a farm wagon drawn by his favourite horses, Brag and Dragon, and lowered, with considerable difficulty, into the family vault.

He had already erected his memorial, which consists of six ten-foot-high slate tablets, inscribed with a history of the Butler family, set in the wall separating St Andrew's churchyard from the grounds of the Abbey House.

The Lawson family, who lived in the Abbey House from 1903 to 1929, experienced dramatic phenomena there. John Cuthbert Lawson, born in 1874, was a fellow of Pembroke College, and an expert on ancient Greece. He served as a naval officer during the First World War and was awarded the OBE for his services to Cambridge University and the War effort. His wife Dorothy was the same age as he, and their four children John, Mary, Jane and Arnold were born between 1901 and 1906.

On the first night the Lawson family stayed in the Abbey House they were frightened by a tremendous banging on a bedroom door. They thought this had been caused by the maid, until she was found cowering under her bedclothes, even more terrified than the children.

Dorothy often felt that somebody was sitting with her in the drawing room, and frequently heard footsteps walking up and down the empty stairs.

An upstairs bedroom was pervaded by something intangible which so disturbed guests that they were unable to sleep properly there. John Cuthbert's brother, a remarkably heavy sleeper, stayed in the bedroom, and complained that he was woken up by something walking around making 'an unholy noise'. Other people in the room below heard noises in the bedroom when it was known to be empty. A servant heard clanking chains there, and voices speaking faintly, which she described as 'so pathetic'.

When the oldest Lawson children, John and Mary, were three and two they began to see a small, furry brown creature, which

5

they called *Wolfie*, running across the nursery on its hind legs. This might have been dismissed as childhood imagination, until their parents began seeing it as well. John Cuthbert called it 'a nondescript kind of animal', while Dorothy identified it as 'a furry thing of light sable colour moving tremendously quickly ... I should say about two feet high'.

From 1906 a figure resembling a nun in her robes would regularly come through John and Dorothy's bedroom, to stand at the foot of her bed, and then cross the room to go behind the curtains. The figure did not frighten every member of the family: the Lawson's eldest child, John, thought of it as a guardian spirit who watched them and the house.

One night Dorothy thought that compassion might help to release the ghost from its earthly confines, and when it entered the room she said: 'In the name of the Holy Trinity, poor soul, rest in peace.' As soon as she said this the figure went to the curtain. It then appeared before John Cuthbert, then before the nurse. Whether, the spectre was a nun, or some other figure, the Lawson family never saw it again.

But the ghosts had not completely departed. Two weeks later Dorothy felt something pulling her out of bed. She told John, in bed with her, to hold her; he pulled her firmly back into the bed. This entity never troubled her again. A few days after that a figure dressed in a full suit of armour briefly appeared before her.

The phantom nun seems not to have abandoned the Abbey House, for Irish labourers who stayed there during the First World War also complained that she disturbed them.

John Cuthbert and Dorothy Lawson both kept records of their experiences at the Abbey House, but they wrote them in secret, and they were not published until many years after their deaths. Yet knowledge of the Abbey House ghosts spread, and the phantom animal was mentioned in Arthur Beale Gray's 1921 guidebook, *Cambridge Revisited*, which observed that it was seen by children rather than adults.

After the Lawson family left the Abbey House their rooms were occupied by Dr Frank Coles Phillips of Corpus Christi College.When he arrived, Dr Phillips did not believe in ghosts. Yet guests staying in the haunted bedroom heard footsteps and felt something moving across the bed. The movements they described followed the same pattern as those noted by the Lawson family, even though the furniture had been rearranged.

Then, in 1931, Dr Phillips saw the phantom animal run along an upstairs floor three nights in a row. He must have left the Abbey House with his scepticism rather dented.

Harold Temperley, who was Master of Peterhouse from 1938 to 1939, rented the southern part of the house, and claimed to know four people who saw ghosts there.

Celia Schofield, who rented the southern part of the house in 1947, had a two-year-old son, Christopher, who said that he could see a 'tiny doggy' there.

Miss Breaman and Miss Young were companions who lived in the southern part of the Abbey House from 1952. During the early nights of her stay Miss Breaman was wakened in the night by a figure hovering over her, or by the paw of an invisible animal pressing on her chest.

Miss Young once awoke to find her bedclothes loose and flapping, and her eiderdown being pulled backwards and forwards over her head. At another time the phantom animal briefly appeared before both Miss Young and Miss Breaman.

The Raynor family moved into the northern part of the house; in 1956 the family's teenage daughter Ashling heard whispering, and once saw the nun reflected in a mirror at the top of the stairs.

Perhaps the strangest phenomenon of all occurred in the spring of 1956 Miss Young had her dog Raggy put to sleep. Raggy used to bounce a ball off a bed and jump after it. One night Mrs Raynor heard a ball being bounced on the floor, followed by the sound of a dog jumping. That night all the dogs in the area howled!

Frederick Stratton, the Professor of Astrophysics in Cambridge University, was interested in the paranormal, and was President of the Society for Psychical Research from 1953 to 1955. He collected manuscripts written by John Cuthbert and Dorothy Lawson, and statements from other tenants of the house, describing their experiences.

The Abbey House may be susceptible to various influences from its past. Possibly the footsteps and the little phantom animal are the spirits of Jacob Butler and his dog, who remained in some way drawn to the house after spending their last days there, while the figure resembling a nun may be in some way connected with Barnwell Priory, the medieval monastery which once stood on the site.

It has been suggested that sometimes young children are susceptible to psychic phenomena which are not so readily observed by adults. This certainly seems to be the case at the Abbey House, where several generations of children, who normally had no knowledge of the history of the house, saw the same phantom animals. It is interesting to read that the Lawson's eldest son thought the phantom nun was a guardian spirit, who was watching them and the house. Perhaps this child sensed that the spirits in the house were harmless, and it might even be possible that they took a protective interest in the house.

Residents seem to have been most likely to experience phenomena soon after moving into the house. The Lawson family recorded much activity during the early years of their tenancy, but they seem to have little to say about activity during the later part of their stay. Possibly new arrivals in a building disturb psychic forces, or perhaps people become in some way acclimatised to a building with the passage of time.

The Archaeology Museum

The University Department of Archaeology in Downing Street contains a museum – one of the city's lesser known museums, yet containing many exhibits of international importance.

T C Lethbridge, the Cambridge-educated archaeologist and psychical researcher, was associated with the museum for many years. He told two ghost stories about the museum in his personal memoir *Ghost and Ghoul* (1962).

There once was a human skull in the museum which was said to jump off tables and shelves in an alarming fashion, and to make exhibits move, or vanish and then re-appear.

Lethbridge tells a more sinister story about a set of witch doctor's bones which were given to the museum. Four small animal bones, each about four inches long, were covered with rough, geometrical patterns and threaded on to a string.

An Englishman who had taken the bones from an African witch doctor died mysteriously after passing them on to a friend. Fearing that the objects might be cursed, the new owner decided to get rid of them to the museum. That same day he died from a burst abscess.

Then another person came to the museum with an identical set of bones. He was frightened because these had similarly been given to him by a friend who had died mysteriously soon afterwards. A few days later people noticed that this man had not left his lodgings. Some colleagues went to his apartment, but the doors and windows were locked. Forcing their way in, they found the man tied up and lying face down on a cushion – suffocated. It was never explained how he could have been bound and smothered in a locked apartment.

THE HAUNTED
BOOKSHOP

The Haunted Bookshop, at 9 St Edward's Passage, is the only building in Cambridge to openly advertise the presence of a ghost. A thriving second-hand business, it acquired its name in 1986 after the proprietor saw a charming apparition at the head of the stairs: an attractive young girl, with long, flowing, fair hair.

This fair-haired girl has since been seen by the present owner, Sara Keys, and some shop staff have followed the girl upstairs, believing her to be a customer, only to find the upper floor empty.

In 1997 a cable channel programme called *The Y Files* made a broadcast from the shop. A psychic on the cast sensed a female presence in the shop, which she identified as a benign entity. Alan Hudleston, a shop assistant, when asked about the ghost, confirmed that the girl had been sighted by other members of staff. He said that her appearances are accompanied by the smell of violets. Evidently this is one ghost that need not be feared: those sighting her may even find the experience pleasing to the senses.

CAMBRIDGE CASTLE

William the Conqueror ordered that a castle be built at Cambridge in 1068. This Castle was rebuilt for Edward I between 1286 and 1296.

Although the castle became the county gaol and administrative centre, it was never an important royal residence or military base, and became obsolete by the fifteenth century. Most of the castle buildings were dismantled over the fifteenth and sixteenth centuries.

The castle was re-fortified during the Civil War, but the fortifications were removed after the War. Only the medieval gatehouse remained in use as a gaol, standing on the east side of Castle Street, north of the modern Castle public house. The gatehouse eventually fell into ruin too, and was demolished in 1842.

The Castle mound still stands, and can be climbed for a panoramic view of the city and the neighbouring countryside.

In 1718 the gatehouse gaol was the setting for dramatic poltergeist activity, which focused on Simon Ockley, the University Professor of Arabic. Simon Ockley clearly possessed a brilliant mind, for he became University Lecturer in Hebrew in 1705, when he was only twenty seven, and Professor of Arabic six years later, at the age of thirty three. But he neglected his financial affairs to concentrate on his studies, with the result that he was imprisoned for debt in the castle in 1718.

Prison life could be very unpleasant in the eighteenth century, but Simon Ockley took care to make friends with the other prisoners, who treated him with some respect. He does not seem to have been kept in unreasonable discomfort, as he was allowed the use of two rooms, and freedom to roam the rest of the gaol and receive visitors. He was also permitted to write

The Gatehouse Gaol

letters, in which he described his experiences.

In April he began to hear rapping noises on his cell walls. These gradually became louder, and by May he was tormented by the sounds of axes cutting wood, trotting horses, or church bells, noises which he described as 'hideous, hollow, inarticulate voices, besides several other inimitable sounds … with an intensity resembling cannonfire'. Loud thumps and bangs came from within the legs of a table in his cell, and his bed was often lifted into the air when he was trying to sleep. Not surprisingly, this kept him awake throughout the night, and prevented him from resting during the day.

Sometimes the noises went into the next room, but they always returned. At other times they decreased, until they sounded like rustling paper in a corner. When this happened Simon Ockley snatched at the curtains or the furniture which seemed to separate him from the noises, hoping he might see if any physical presence was causing the sounds, but when he did so a forceful gust of wind drove him back.

Even his privacy was not respected. When he went to what he described as the 'house of office' he was surrounded by the noises of smashing wood. Convinced that the other prisoners were playing tricks on him, he would run from the room – only to find the connecting rooms empty, and the other prisoners asleep. He took to holding the door, and pushing it open when any noises began, but the room outside was always empty.

Ockley regarded himself as an educated and enlightened man. He wrote that he did not believe in witchcraft, and he was sceptical about the existence of ghosts, but he found himself unable to explain what was taking place, and why this should happen to him. His daughter visited him, and observed the phenomena for herself. Another visitor laughed at his story, whereupon the whole room was suddenly filled with vibrations which nearly threw them off their chairs.

Fortunately for Simon Ockley, his friends secured his release in June. But in July he was at his home at Swavesey, a village to the north-west of Cambridge, when he and his daughter heard a loud noise upstairs. They rushed to the upper floor, but the rooms were empty. He may have been free of his captivity, but he was not free of his phantom tormentors. He died little more than two years later, in 1720, a frightened and haunted man.

Although little effort had been made to systematically analyse psychic activity in the eighteenth century, Simon Ockley's experiences resemble manifestations of what has since been termed 'poltergeist' activity.

The word poltergeist is German and means noisy spirit. Typically it is characterised by psychic disturbances, when inexplicable noises are heard. These often begin as rappings on walls or furniture, and then grow in intensity. Objects are then moved, or even thrown through the air, without any obvious cause.

Poltergeist activity is often associated with a person, rather than a place, and may follow this person around. Many victims of this type of activity are suffering from stress or anxiety, and it has been suggested that this in some way releases unconscious psychic forces (*see* St John's College).

Like many victims of poltergeist activity, Simon Ockley was clearly suffering from great stress and anxiety when the incidents took place. Being imprisoned for debt cannot have been a pleasant experience, neither did he enjoy his experiences, and wished they would stop. Friends and acquaintances suggested that the happenings might have been a product of his imagination; Ockley considered this possibility, but was unable to convince himself that this was the case. He took some measures to detect trickery, but to no avail, and he emphasised that the noises he heard were 'inimitable', and could not easily have been created by the other prisoners, or even within his own imagination

Simon Ockley may have been an eccentric person with strange habits, but he was also a highly educated man, with an incisive academic mind and, whatever explanation may be offered for his experience, it genuinely disturbed him at the time – and for the rest of his life.

CHRIST'S COLLEGE

Alfred Ponsford Baker, a graduate of Christ's, used the college as the setting for a novel entitled *A College Mystery*. Published in 1918, this tells how the ghost of Christopher Round came to haunt Christ's College. A work of fiction, it has been widely accepted as true.

Born in Delgoa Bay, South Africa, in 1873, Alfred Ponsford Baker studied at Christ's from 1892 to 1895, and became a writer and history lecturer at Cambridge. He died in 1919, and is commemorated by a plaque in the college chapel.

The most beautiful features of Christ's College include the seventeenth-century Fellows' Building, and the attractive Fellows' Garden which is noted for a picturesque bathing pool. Much of the activity in *A College Mystery* centres on the Fellows' Building and Garden.

Early in the nineteenth century Christopher Round went to

Philip Collier's Rooms in the Fellows' Building

Cambridge to take a classics degree. Here he made the acquaintance of another freshman, Philip Collier, who was noted for his good looks and charming personality. Round was the harder worker, with a sound grasp of his subject, but he lacked Collier's grace and style. Consequently Collier won awards at every academic contest, while Round could only secure an honourable mention.

After taking their degrees Round and Collier were elected Fellows of Christ's College, and given apartments in the Fellows' Building. Soon afterwards, Philip Collier was nominated to become Professor of Greek, above the more methodical Christopher Round. At the same time both men fell in love with a woman called Mary Clifford but, to Christopher Round's disappointment, she chose Philip Collier's offer of marriage.

Collier began to neglect his duties and avoid his colleagues, disappearing from Christ's College for lengthy periods, and returning to lock himself in his apartment in the Fellows' Building. He was frequently observed to be unkempt and dishevelled, smelling of spirits, reeling and staggering in an ungainly fashion, his speech slurred.

Christopher Round imagined that he was losing Mary Clifford and a Professorship to an irresponsible drunkard. One night Round was walking past the pond in the Fellows' Garden when Collier came staggering towards him with an unsteady gait. Suddenly, Collier stumbled and fell into the pond. Round then noticed a pole lying on the ground; picking it up he extended it to Collier. But then Round was overcome with anger and jealousy. Why should he rescue a drunken scoundrel who was about to cheat him out of his Professorship, and the woman he loved? He raised the pole, and furiously struck Collier about the head.

Round then returned to the Fellows' Building. The next morning, the local newspapers reported that Collier's body had

The pool in the Fellows' Garden

been found at the end of the Fellows' Garden. An inquest returned a verdict of accidental death. Mary Clifford, heartbroken, left Cambridge, never to return.

Christopher Round later discovered that Mary Clifford had been suffering from a serious illness, but that her life might have been saved by an operation. At that time surgical operations were very painful and dangerous, but some doctors were experimenting with a new medical process called anaesthesia.

Nowadays anaesthetics are routinely used to relieve pain in medical operations, but in early Victorian times they were a new invention and little was known about them. Philip Collier had been trying to find an anaesthetic which might help Mary Clifford, and in his desperation to help her, had been taking anaesthetics himself. This explained his unusual behaviour. By killing Philip Collier, Christopher Round had taken away the best chance of saving his beloved Mary's life.

Christopher Round spent the rest of his life at Christ's College, a lonely figure, immersing himself in his studies, shunning company and refusing all offers of promotion. He never mentioned Philip Collier or Mary Clifford in conversation, but the guilt preyed on his mind so greatly that he wrote a confession, which he gave to a solicitor in a sealed envelope to be opened fifty years after his death.

Yet there was an anomaly in his confession. The obituaries of Philip Collier agreed that his body was found at the end of the Fellows' Garden, away from the pond. Did Christopher Round's confession contain the full truth? Did Collier struggle from the pond, and die from cold and exposure, rather than from a blow to the head? Did Round murder Collier, and then try and soothe his conscience by inventing a story in which he was not fully to blame for his rival's death? Did Collier die as a result of his medical experiments, and was Round so obsessed with jealousy that he only *imagined* himself to blame for his rival's death? Did the University authorities, fearing a scandal, seek to conceal the real circumstances? When Christopher Round's confession was

The figure of a man on Fellows' Garden

18

published it was too late to re-investigate the case.

Since then, members of Christ's College have seen an elderly man walk across the Fellows' Garden. He wears an old fashioned swallow-tailed coat and a beaver hat which conceals his face, but he conveys an air of care and unhappiness. Always avoiding the pond, he vanishes into the shadows at the end of the garden. Witnesses affirm that his appearances are preceded or followed by the sound of footsteps on the staircase of the Fellows' Building, and the sound of a door opening and closing in the chambers which Christopher Round occupied. But when they look the passage is empty.

The story of Christopher Round has circulated widely, and sightings of the phantom don have been reported in Peter Underwood's *Gazetteer of British Ghosts* (1971); Andrew Green's *Our Haunted Kingdom* (1973); and John Brooks's *Good Ghost Guide* (1994).

The present authors suspect that the story may have been attached to a genuine apparition from the Victorian era which has been seen in parts of central Cambridge but whose real identity remains a mystery.

CORPUS CHRISTI COLLEGE

Corpus Christi College was established in 1352 and built around a courtyard, known as Old Court, which now forms the oldest complete college courtyard at either Oxford or Cambridge. The name Corpus Christi, Latin for The Body of Christ, derives from the guild of Corpus Christi, the organisation that founded the college.

The old-fashioned lodge, which occupied the eastern half of the south range of Old Court, was the setting for two sinister tragedies.

Dr John Spencer became master of Corpus in 1667. His daughter Elizabeth was born in 1672. Two years later, in 1674,

The old Master's Lodge

Dr Spencer's wife died, and was buried in St Benet's church, next to the college.

When Elizabeth was sixteen she fell in love with a student called James Betts, but Dr Spencer considered him unsuitable for his daughter.

At the end of term, Elizabeth was enjoying James Betts's company in the Master's Lodge when she heard her father coming up the stairs. Fearful of Dr Spencer's anger, both for Elizabeth and himself, James Betts hid in a cupboard, not knowing that this cupboard could be opened only by a secret spring which could not be released from the inside.

Dr Spencer may have suspected that Elizabeth had been entertaining James Betts, the student for whom he felt such great animosity. Perhaps it was then that he devised a plan to end their affair once and for all. Drawing Elizabeth from the room, he ordered her to accompany him on a journey which kept them away from Cambridge for the vacation.

After Dr Spencer returned to Corpus, nobody dared to open the cupboard, terrified of what they might find, and fearful that they might be accused of culpability in a horrible crime. Heartbroken at the loss of her love, Elizabeth died within a few months, and was buried in St Benet's church on 9 December 1688.

Dr Spencer's position at the University was such that nobody dared to suggest that he was in any way involved with James Betts's disappearance, but who knows what guilt he must have felt with the death of his only daughter, and her lover, on his conscience. Dying an unhappy and guilt-ridden man five years later, he was buried with his family in St Benet's church.

When another Master came to the college, he opened the cupboard, and was shocked and terrified to find a skeleton inside.

Dr Henry Butts was another master of Corpus who met a tragic end. Dr Butts was appointed Master in 1626. Shortly afterwards there was a plague outbreak in Cambridge. While many members of the University fled the town for safety, he stayed to care for the sick and dying. He wrote: 'Myself am alone, a destitute and forsaken man, not a scholar with me in the college, not a scholar seen by me without'. The experience affected him deeply, and he acquired a ghost-like look which remained even after the plague had abated.

Another slight on his sensitive nature was to weigh even heavier on his mind. In 1632 King Charles I visited Cambridge with Queen Henrietta Maria. It was customary for the University to stage a play during royal visits, but Dr Butts disagreed with the master of Trinity College, Dr Thomas Comber, over which play to show. They eventually arranged for two authors to write different plays which were staged on separate occasions.

The play sponsored by Dr Comber was a sensational success, applauded and praised, but the play supported by Dr Butts was a dismal flop. It was booed down by the audience, and the Vice-Chancellor of the University reprimanded Dr Butts for allowing it to be staged. This so upset Dr Butts that he hanged himself in the Master's Lodge ten days later.

A new Master's Lodge was built at Corpus Christi in 1832. The lower floor of the Old Lodge where Dr Spencer and Dr Butts had lived then became college kitchens, while the upper floors became accommodation for students and staff.

It has been suggested that the latent psychic energy contained in an old building can be tapped if the building is altered, as if the alterations awaken dormant spirits. After the conversion of the Old Lodge in the Old Court, strange and inexplicable footsteps and banging noises began to be heard there. Rumours of ghostly activity circulated. Porcheron and Body, the college cooks, were convinced that a ghost lurked in the kitchens, and no college servant would stay in the kitchens at night. The Fellows ascribed this to over-active imagination, but the kitchen staff were adamant that the noises they heard were quite unlike kitchen equipment heating or cooling down. Tales were told of students who had been frightened by an apparition of the upper part of a man floating in the air, and once an undergraduate was said to have fled terrified after seeing a head without a body.

A student called Walter Moule, who later became a missionary in China, had rooms in the Old Lodge during 1883, where he often heard loud banging like a trap door falling, or maybe the opening of the trap on a gallows. The college authorities were ready to dismiss this as rumour or gossip until one fateful day when Walter Moule's uncle, Charles Moule, a senior Fellow of the college, experienced something which terrified him beyond reason. Several witnesses saw Charles Moule in broad daylight crawling out of his rooms on his hands and knees in total terror. Extremely frightened, not to mention deeply embarrassed by the encounter, Charles Moule never revealed what had scared him so horribly.

In the Easter Term of 1903 Llewellyn Powys, a student who later became a prominent writer, lived on the west side of Old Court, opposite the Old Lodge.

One afternoon he was in his rooms when he was seized by a feeling of unease. Looking out of his window he saw the head and shoulders of a long-haired man leaning from a dormer window at the top of the Old Lodge. Llewellyn Powys watched it for three minutes, while it remained quite motionless. He then ran to another room for a better view but by then the long-haired man had disappeared.

Running across the courtyard, Llewellyn Powys found the upper rooms of the Old Lodge locked; he later established that the student who lived there had been away that afternoon, taking the only key to the rooms with him.

The following autumn term a student living in the Old Lodge was woken in the night by the wash stand at the foot of his bed shaking and knocking violently. At 5 am one dark morning an occupant of another room woke to find the figure of a man standing by his bedside. At first motionless, the figure then glided across the bedroom and through the shut door. The same student was later awakened by continual noises which were so loud and disconcerting that he went to a friend in another room, asking for his company to support him. The two friends returned to find the rooms empty and silent. When the friend left the student returned to his bedroom. On opening the door he saw a shadowy figure standing by his bed. He fled his rooms in terror, refusing point blank to stay there any longer.

Events at Corpus Christi reached a climax in October 1904, when a student called Arthur Wade took lodgings on the middle floor of the Old Lodge. Arthur Wade had made friends with two students from King's College called Shane Leslie and John Capron. Shane Leslie was a member of an aristocratic Irish family, and a cousin of Winston Churchill.

The three students shared an interest in the supernatural, and had formed an amateur psychical research group. Deciding to drive the ghosts from the Old Lodge, they obtained an English translation of a medieval exorcism ceremony. Entering Arthur Wade's room at ten o'clock at night, John Capron called on the spirit to appear. To their amazement a mist formed, which gradually assumed the outline of a

Ghost Hunt in the Master's Lodge

24

human body. John Capron cried: 'the thing is here' and as Shane Leslie watched in fascination he felt his hair beginning to rise. John Capron then approached the shape, with Arthur Wade and Shane Leslie standing behind him, but all three felt themselves forced backwards. The shape disappeared; then re-appeared in the dark frame of the open doorway, where it took on the form of a man, visible from the knees upwards, wearing a seventeenth-century costume with a ruff collar and lace cuffs, hanging as though in punishment or torment.

As the three amateur exorcists stood in terror some other students, alarmed by the noises they had heard from the Old Lodge, broke into the room. They were in time to see the entity dematerialise.

John Capron then cried that he saw the spirit going upstairs. Gathering their remaining strength, Capron, Wade and Leslie led the other students upstairs, where they charged into the room at the top of the staircase, which belonged to a medical student called Milner.

This student, who was a self-confessed atheist, was angry at this intrusion, but then collapsed on the floor, muttering: 'I am cold, I am icy cold'. Milner's room was filled with a scene of muddled confusion. Capron, Wade and Leslie were psychologically and physically exhausted, Milner was writhing on the floor as if possessed, and the other students in the room were frightened out of their wits. Milner, Capron, Wade and Leslie were led away to see the college doctor, and the college chaplain.

The exorcism became the talk of Cambridge. For several months people went to Old Court to watch the Old Lodge for any further manifestations of spiritual activity, and practical jokers sometimes appeared in the windows dressed in sheets. The College authorities were rather angry about the affair, not only because they thought it brought unwelcome publicity, but also because several undergraduates pulled the panelling off the Lodge walls in a search for evil spirits.

None of the participants in the exorcism suffered any permanent ill effects, but Hugh Milner possessed a more spiritual attitude for the rest of his life. John Capron became a church of England clergyman, while Shane Leslie became a convinced believer in the supernatural, writing several highly regarded books on the subject.

A woman in her sixties who came on the Cambridge Ghost Walk said that she had attended a Catholic girl's school in the 1940s, where Shane Leslie had been a frequent visitor. She recalled him as 'a tall spare man who told us stories that gave us nightmares for weeks'.

John Capron, Arthur Wade and Shane Leslie may have released the latent spiritual energy in the Old Lodge, for there were no further reports of ghosts there.

But then, in 1999, a party of students from the USA staying in the Old Lodge reported to the Cambridge Ghost Walk that they had heard knocking sounds in the building.

A document about Dr Butt's suicide was discovered some years after the exorcism. It said that he had hanged himself in a doorframe by the staircase in the Master's Lodge, and he was found with his knees dragging on the floor, so that his body appeared to be cut off at the knees – in the place and in the posture in which the students had seen his apparition.

CROMWELL LODGE

The house at number four Trumpington Street is now divided between a restaurant and a language school. During the late Victorian period, when this building was known as Cromwell Lodge, it was the scene of psychic activity.

Mrs Jephson, who occupied the house at the time, frequently heard footsteps going up and down the stairs between one o'clock and four o'clock in the morning. Yet whenever anybody looked out on to the staircase there was nothing to be seen. At other times footsteps ran around the top floor when it was known that nobody was there.

A servant called Emma Ellis was going to bed at 10 o'clock one night when she saw a girl wearing a hood standing by the door. The girl was very beautiful, yet Emma was so unnerved to have seen the figure that she screamed and fainted. When she came round the hooded girl had vanished.

The entities that haunted Cromwell Lodge could sometimes be benign spirits. Once Mrs Jephson's son was travelling in Scotland, and she was anxious for his welfare. She was awakened at midnight by the touch of a cold, clammy hand; when she opened her eyes she saw a beautiful, ethereal face with piercing oval eyes staring at her. The figure communicated that her son was safe. Within a few days she received a letter from her son who was indeed safe and well in Perth.

Between 1889 and 1892 Mrs Jephson took in a lodger, a University graduate called Mr Joy, who often heard bells ringing in the house between one and two o'clock in the morning. In 1895, Joy came back to stay for a few days, bringing his friend Mr Hadath. They asked to stay in separate rooms and, in a special show of bravery, Hadath asked to stay in Joy's old room.

That night Joy and Hadath both heard rattling, like crockery shaking and breaking. Each kept accusing the other of playing the fool. Eventually they both heard the noises together. Then the bells in the house began ringing, described by Hadath as: 'bells of many varieties of tone and strength, it seemed as if every one in the house was ringing'.

The cacophony awoke Mrs Jephson and her dog, who came into the hall. Then the bells stopped ringing, to be followed by a silence perhaps more ominous than any noise. Then there was a loud repetitive clanging, like metal being beaten. This was too much for the dog, who shot to the wall, cowering in terror. Perhaps Joy and Hadath maintained a more rational appearance, but they too were terrified, and even after the noises had stopped they found themselves unable to sleep.

Next morning both men left Cromwell Lodge, never to return, despite their long-standing connections with Cambridge, but they sent sworn affidavits of their experiences to the Society for Psychical Research.

Perhaps the mystery of Cromwell Lodge was partly solved when the house changed ownership in 1899. While it was being renovated, three human skulls – two male and one female – were found under the dining room window. Perhaps the spirits of the deceased had troubled the house. The skulls were removed to the University Museum of Archaeology.

No further activity has been reported at Cromwell Lodge, and people living there now have witnessed no supernatural phenomena.

Mrs Jephson's affidavit has a strange aspect, which is telling for later psychical research. She reported seeing 'a beautiful, ethereal figure with piercing oval eyes staring at her'. This character's appearance sounds very similar to figures reported in the recent stories told by people who claim to have been abducted by UFOs.

At that time, UFO sightings were not as commonly reported

as they are today. (UFO sightings have become increasingly frequent since the Second World War, and the term flying saucer was first used in 1947.) But perhaps Mrs Jephson saw an archetypal ghost figure whose appearances were subject to other interpretations in an age before space travel was a scientific possibility.

CUTTER FERRY PATH

This was the scene of reliably attested ghost sightings.

People were once ferried across the Cam at Midsummer Common. One of the ferries, Cutter's Ferry, was replaced by the Pye Bridge, an iron footbridge, in 1927. The ferry is commemorated by Cutter Ferry Path on the north side of the River.

There was a dank, marshy clump of woodland known as The Willows to the north of Cutter Ferry Path, between the modern Manhattan Drive and Elizabeth Way. On 17 December 1927 a ghost was sighted here.

The ghost was seen again on New Year's Eve. After this it made repeated evening appearances, and by the middle of January 1928 it had become a subject of conversation among the townsfolk and students. The Willows was partly flooded at the time, and the damp, forlorn nature of the spot, combined with the nocturnal cries of a colony of owls who lived in the trees, must have intensified the location's eerie atmosphere.

One young woman was walking along Cutter Ferry Path on 20 January when she saw a luminous body three feet high bobbing up and down in the middle of the pool. She told press reporters: 'Although it was pitch black night it was perfectly visible. It went to the bank and then returned to the water. I rubbed my eyes, but I was not mistaken, and by the time I reached the end of the lane I was running.'

A young man saw the ghost hovering around The Willows in a circular pattern, over an area forty yards around an old tree stump: 'It takes a wide course, then seems to come towards you with the speed of an express train, only to stop by the old stump. It always vanished into the same thick bush. At a distance it appears to be of a triangular shape, tapering towards the ground, and a little nearer there is distinctly to be seen the cowl of a hooded monk. Another time it was a good impression of a bent old man with a stick, varying from five to eight feet in height. It gives you a most wonderful feeling of fascination.'

Some people claimed to see the ghost drifting across the river from the Abbey House, (which may not have been inappropriate, as it had been compared to a monk in his robes).

By the middle of January a many as fifty people might gather at The Willows at night-time, hoping for a glimpse of the ghost A boy scout troop decided to embark on a spot of ghost-hunting one evening, but the ghost failed to make an appearance.

Hoaxers were eventually attracted to the area. One practical joker painted a face on a box, and placed it on a tree branch with a sheet hanging from it, but this was quickly recognised. Another mischief maker came to The Willows one night dressed in a sheet but he, too, was recognised, and people threw things at him.

This throws an interesting side-light on some famous hauntings. It has been suggested that auto-suggestion might account for some sightings, and that phenomena might even be created by practical jokers, but even the most gullible amateur ghost-hunters have little difficulty in recognising trickery and treating it as such.

Heavy rainfall at the end of January seems to have discouraged ghost-hunters for a while, and sightings of the ghost passed with the onset of summer.

The area has since been drained. Although it is still open land, there are fewer trees there, and the ghost has not been spotted recently.

Even in 1928 many people believed that the mysterious light was simply a discharge of marsh gas, or will-o'-the wisp. But the mysterious nature of the lights obviously left a great impression on those who saw them.

EMMANUEL COLLEGE

Emmanuel House, which stood on the south of the College grounds, against Parker Street, was the focus of ghostly activity. Witnesses of the events were interviewed by the Society for Psychical Research, and details were filed in the society's archives.

Emmanuel College

The Harris family, who took up residence in 1867, often heard footsteps running down empty passageways. In 1870 Emily Harris, the mother of the family, was in bed when she saw a female figure standing by the bed wearing a grey veil. Thinking it might have been a trick of the light, she moved around in the bed, but the figure remained stationary, yet quite distinct. At this point she dived under the bedclothes, too frightened even to scream! When she eventually looked out again the figure had disappeared.

On employing a young boy as a servant, the Harris family

were careful not to tell him that Emmanuel House was haunted, but one morning, a few days after his arrival, he was heard screaming. The whole household ran to see what was wrong, and found him huddled on the floor in a terrified heap, crying that he had just seen a ghost His description of the ghost corresponded exactly with the figure which Emily Harris had seen.

Miss Bowen, who was the next tenant to rent Emmanuel Lodge after the Harris family, continued to hear the footsteps, as did her maid, Kate.

When Miss Bowen left the Lodge it became a girls' boarding school. In 1884 a teacher called Miss Bellamy, who was respected as a particularly formidable no-nonsense schoolmistress, was standing in the kitchen when a strange lady came down the stairs and crossed the hall. Miss Bellamy was particularly puzzled for the lady, who had not been seen to enter the house, had an unfamiliar appearance, and was gliding along the floor without making any noise or movement, apparently unaware that she was being watched by a respected schoolmistress. The lady passed from view, heading towards the dining room, but when Miss Bellamy went to look for her the lady had vanished, and nobody had seen her leave the house.

Unlike the two previous occupants of the Lodge who had seen the ghost, Miss Bellamy remained quite calm and composed, and talked about the sighting with a clear mind. She did not find out that the house was supposed to be haunted until some years later. The Harris family knew of a vague tradition that three previous occupants of Emmanuel Lodge had committed suicide. There is a possibility that some disturbing events had affected the building, but the Harris family had few details about this tradition.

Emmanuel Lodge was demolished in 1893 to make way for the present Lodge, and no ghostly activity has been noted on the site since.

The Folk Museum

The Cambridge and County Folk Museum, in Castle Street, is housed in a sixteenth century building, which was the White Horse Inn until 1934.

The Folk Museum was opened in 1936, and contains a fascinating collection of items connected with local life and customs. Enid Porter, curator of the Museum from 1947 to 1976, was an outstanding collector of folktales, including many ghost stories. In 1969 she published the results of her research in *Cambridgeshire Customs and Folklore,* a fascinating book and a mine of information about life and beliefs in the area.

Early in the twentieth century, when the building was still the White Horse Inn, a secret room was discovered. It was noticed that a window in the north wall did not connect with any room inside the building. After further investigation it was found that there was a small hidden chamber in a space between the ground floor and the first floor.

It was suggested that this chamber could have been a secret hideaway, where highwaymen staying at the Inn could take shelter to evade their pursuers. Unfortunately, the chamber had to be removed to make way for a staircase.

There is a tradition that the ghost of a soldier in Civil War uniform can be seen standing at the top of the staircase, where the secret room used to be. Cambridge was used as a base by the Roundheads during the Civil War. Although no actual fighting took place in Cambridge, the Castle earthworks, a short distance from the Folk Museum, were re-fortified out of fear that the town might come under attack from supporters of Charles I. It is therefore possible that soldiers may have been billeted in the White Horse Inn. Unfortunately, none of the present museum staff has seen the phantom soldier

However, unexplained footsteps have been heard in the upper part of the building as recently as 1996..

The exhibits in the folk museum include good luck charms, and items which were believed to bestow good or bad fortune on the owner or the recipient. Some of these can be seen in Room Seven, devoted to life in the Fens, where there is a display of objects which were placed in local houses to protect the inhabitants against witchcraft and evil spirits.

THE GOGMAGOG HILLS

The Gogmagog Hills, four-and-a-half miles south of Cambridge on the A1307 rise to a height of 234 feet (71 metres) above sea level, making them by far the highest point in Cambridgeshire.

The Cambridge Preservation Society runs the Gogmagog Hills as a country park and nature reserve. Covering 110 acres, with four miles of footpaths and nature trails, 'The Gogs' is a pleasant place in which to enjoy the delights of the countryside.

The Hills are topped by a circular ditch and rampart known as Wandlebury. About 900 feet in diameter, they occupy fifteen acres. Archaeological excavation suggests that the earthworks were dug in the third century BC, then re-dug on a larger scale at the start of the Christian era. The earthworks were probably made by the Iceni, the Iron Age people who ruled East Anglia before the Roman Conquest, but they ceased to be inhabited after Roman times.

The name Wandlebury derives from the Anglo-Saxon: Wandil's Fort. Wandil, or Vandil, seems to have been an important figure in dark-age mythology. He was a giant and a sea king; a supernatural figure – possibly even a God – who the early Anglo-Saxons often associated with the great monuments from Roman or Prehistoric times.

The name Gogmagog is of recent origin, dating only from the sixteenth century. Gog and Magog appear in the Bible as fearsome giants, while medieval English legend identified them as the last survivors of a race of giants who once lived in Britain.

Wandlebury is the subject of a ghost story, first recorded in 1211 by Gervase of Tilbury. Gervase, who was probably born at Tilbury in Essex in the second half of the twelfth century, travelled around Europe as a scholar and a diplomat. In 1211 he wrote the *Otia Imperialia*, a collection of the stories and anecdotes which he had heard during his life.

One tale describes how a knight called Osbert Fitzhugh rode from Cambridge to challenge the ghost of Wandlebury. The story was translated from the original Latin by Arthur Gray, master of Jesus College – who was also a writer of ghost stories (*see* Jesus College) – and is quoted in full.

In England … there is a town named Cambridge, in the neighbour-hood of which there is a place called Wandlebury … on the hill top, there is a level space surrounded with entrenchments and with a single entrance like a gate. There is a very ancient tradition, attested by popular report, that if a warrior enters this level space at dead of night, when the moon is shining, and calls 'knight to knight come forth', immediately he will be confronted by a warrior, armed for fight, who, charging horse to horse, either dismounts his adversary or is dismounted.

But I should state that the warrior must enter the enclosure alone, though his companions may look on from outside. As proof of the truth of this I quote a story told to me by the country people of the neighbourhood.

There was in Great Britain, not many days ago, a knight redoubtable in arms and possessed of every noble quality, among the barons second in power to few, to none in worth. His name was Osbert Fitzhugh. One day he came as a guest to the town I have mentioned [Cambridge] and, it being winter time, after supper, as is the fashion with great folk, he was sitting in the evening by the fireside in the family of his wealthy host, listening to tales of exploits of ancient days; and while he gave ear to them it chanced that one of the people of the country mentioned the wondrous legend aforesaid.

The brave man resolved to make personal trial of the truth of what he was told. So he selected one of his noble squires, and, attended by him, went to the place. In complete armour he came to the appointed spot, mounted his steed, and, dismissing his attendant, entered the camp alone. He cried aloud to discover his opponent, and in response a knight, or what looked like a knight, came forth to meet him, similarly armed, as it seemed. Well, with shields advanced and levelled lances they charged, and each horseman sustained his opponent's shock. But Osbert parried the spear-thrust of his antagonist, and with a powerful blow struck him to the ground. He was on his feet again in an instant, and, seeing that Osbert was leading off the horse by the bridle, as the spoils of conquest, he poised his lance, and hurling it like a javelin, with a violent effort he pierced Osbert's thigh.

Our knight, however, in the exultation of his victory, either did not feel or did not regard the wound, and his adversary having disappeared, he came out of the camp victorious, and gave the horse which he had won to his squire. It was tall, active and beautiful to behold.

He was met on his return by a number of the family, who marvelled at the tale, were delighted at the overthrow of the knight, and loudly applauded the bravery of the illustrious baron.

When Osbert took off his arms and discarded his iron greaves he saw one of them filled with clotted blood. The family were amazed at the wound, but the Knight scorned fear.

The neighbours, aroused from slumber, came thronging together, and their growing marvel induced them to keep watch.

As evidence of the victory the horse was kept, still tethered. It was displayed to public view with its fierce eyes, erect neck, and black mane; its knightly saddle and all its trappings were likewise black. At cockcrow the horse, prancing, snorting and pawing the earth, suddenly burst its reins and regained its native liberty. It fled, vanished, and none could trace it.

And our noble knight had a perpetual reminder of the wound which he had sustained, in that each year, as the same night returned, the wound, though apparently cured and closed, opened again. So it came about that the famous warrior, some years later, went over the sea, and, after performing many deeds of valour against the heathen, by God's will ended his days.

Gervase's narrative suggests that he had visited Wandlebury, for he gives a reasonable description of the hill fort.

Stories about an encounter between a knight and a supernatural warrior, in a mysterious ancient site, were popular with medieval audiences, and appear in the legends of King Arthur.

Gervase's story is interesting for the details it gives about life in the middle ages. He shows how a medieval knight might have enjoyed hospitality in Cambridge, and how two knights might engage in combat.

The phantom of Wandlebury was not a very chivalrous opponent: it broke the rules of a tournament – and basic fair play – by striking an opponent from behind when the combat was supposed to be over.

In many tales of an encounter with an other-worldly realm, the hero often acquires a wonderful possession – in this case a horse – which is then lost or snatched away. But the hero is sometimes left with a mysterious wound or scar as a permanent reminder of his adventure.

Osbert FitzHugh also gained a special place in history. He can be regarded as the first Cambridge ghost hunter, for he was the first person who took advantage of a visit to Cambridge to seek an encounter with the supernatural.

Jesus College

Arthur Gray, who was Master of Jesus College from 1912 to 1940, wrote the official history of the College. He also wrote a series of ghost stories with Cambridge settings*. Many of Arthur Gray's ghost stories were set in Jesus College, being cleverly written around its historic architectural features, and incorporating events and persons from the college's history.

In 1919 he published some of his ghost stories under the pseudonym *Ingulphus*, with the title *Brief Tedious Tales of Granta* and *Gramarye*. A ghost story enthusiast might find it enjoyable to visit Jesus College with a copy of this book, and read it while exploring places mentioned in the tales.

Arthur Gray's best-known ghost story is the tale of The Everlasting Club, written about *G* Staircase of Jesus College, which was traditionally known as 'Cow Lane', although nobody knew why. An odd feature of *G* Staircase was an empty study, which was always kept locked.

In 1911 Arthur Gray wrote a story to explain why this room had been closed. He told it to various students, and it proved so popular that it passed into college tradition even before it was published.

Arthur Gray said that he had seen the register of The Everlasting Club, which was founded in 1738 by Alan Dermot, an Irish nobleman studying at Cambridge. Charles Belassis – who was a historically documented member of Jesus College – and five other young Cambridge men joined the Everlasting Club.

Alan Dermot framed the club rules. All seven members would be called Everlastings. They would be Corporeal

* He should not be confused with Arthur Beales Gray, the Cambridge printer who wrote *Cambridge Revisited*, (1921).

40

Everlastings during their lifetimes, and remain members after death as Incorporeal Everlastings.

The Everlasting Club's annual meeting would take place on 2 November – All Souls' Day. Any Everlasting failing to attend would be punished – the precise word in the register was 'mulcted' – by Alan Dermot.

Club meetings were notorious for drunkenness and debauchery. All manner of riotous behaviour took place, and the sounds of drunken carousing and ribald blasphemy echoed across Jesus College.

This continued until 1743, when one Everlasting called Henry Davenport left Cambridge to serve as a soldier with the British army, which was then campaigning in Germany.

Entrance to Charles Belassis's study – final rendezvous of the Everlasting Club

The Everlasting Club register showed that Alan Dermot attended the meeting on All Souls' Day in 1743, because it contained his signature under that date, and other messages in his handwriting, including a note that Henry Davenport would be mulcted for non-attendance.

A week later the Everlastings received the news that, on 28 October, five days before the All Souls' Day meeting, Alan Dermot had fought a duel with somebody who objected to his wicked ways. Alan Dermot had lost the combat and been killed. He had attended the meeting as an Incorporeal Member!

The Everlastings then received the news that Henry Davenport had been killed by a cannon shot on 3 November. Alan Dermot was capable of carrying out punishments from beyond the grave!

Over the next few years the other Everlastings died in mysterious circumstances, until 1766, when only Charles Belassis was left. When All Souls' Day arrived he locked himself in his study, on the Staircase known as Cow Lane, hoping that he might escape Alan Dermot's anger.

That night from ten o'clock, there was a hideous uproar in Charles Belassis's study. 'Blasphemous outcries and ribald songs, such as had not been heard for twenty years, aroused from sleep or study the occupants of the court.'

At midnight all noise ceased, and the lights in Charles Belassis's study went out. Next morning the room was in total chaos, with books arid furniture strewn around the room, and glasses and bottles littering the floor.

In the centre of the room there was a table surrounded by seven chairs. Six were empty, but in the seventh chair sat, Charles Belassis, stone dead, his head thrown back and his face paralysed in a look of horrified terror.

On the table lay the register of The Everlasting Club, signed by all seven original members including Alan Dermot, in their own handwriting, with a final message that Charles Belassis had been mulcted for failing to provide proper hospitality.

Charles Belassis's study was locked, and never used again. Few people dared to enter, but it was said that every 2 November, from ten o'clock until midnight, lights came on in the window, and the sound of drunken revelry echoed from the room as it had in the days of The Everlasting Club.

The study on Cow Lane was re-opened in 1924, and has remained in use ever since. But the story of The Everlasting Club was such a popular part of college folklore that it is mentioned in the 1979 re-publication of Arthur Gray's college history.

On 2 November 1977 a student social club called The Jesus Old Contemptibles held an evening meal in the room on Cow Lane, with the hope that they might see the members of The Everlasting Club. No unexpected guests appeared. Perhaps this was just as well, considering what happened to Charles Belassis on the night of 2 November 1766!

The story of The Everlasting Club may have been inspired by another Cambridge society: the Ghost Club. This society was founded at Trinity College in 1851, laujched publicly in London in 1862, and revived in 1882 (*see* Trinity College).

The archives of the revived Ghost Club were deposited in the British Museum Library in 1936, on the understanding that they would not be opened for 25 years. Thus they are now open to readers. The revised club rules, as framed in 1882, said that anybody joining the club became a 'Ghost', and, like the Everlastings, they remained a member in this life and the afterlife. Like the Everlasting Club, the Ghost Club's annual meeting was held on 2 November, chosen in this case because of the French tradition of visiting cemeteries to pay respects to deceased ancestors on that day.

Meetings were held to honour all ghosts and all members, living and dead, were cordially invited to attend. Another telling detail in the rules was the expression that any ghost infringing club regulations would be mulcted by the organisation.

Arthur Gray possessed an interest in the supernatural. Evidently he knew of the revived Ghost Club: he may even have been a member, and this might have caused him to write the story of the Everlasting Club.

KING STREET

At the start of the twentieth century a family took lodgings in a house in King Street. The mother soon noticed that her two young sons were sad and nervous in the house, but she could not persuade them to tell her why.

Then, late on a winter's night, she heard a loud thump from the boys' bedroom, followed by the sound of furiously running footsteps. The mother and father rushed to the bedroom, and burst through the door, where they found the younger son collapsed on the floor and the older boy trembling in the corner. After the children were calmed and reassured they said that since they had moved into the house, they had heard footsteps running around the room, but they saw nothing.

The parents asked other King Street residents about the house, and were told that it had been occupied by an old miser who stayed in that one room, and constantly ran around looking into each corner to see that nobody had taken his money. The miser was so attached to the room where he kept his money that his presence remained there after his death.

King's College

King's College is famous for its chapel, one of the great masterpieces of English architecture built during the fifteenth and sixteenth centuries.

The college's other features include The Gibbs Building. Built in 1723, this stands on the west side of the main college courtyard, facing the River Cam.

The Chapel and Gibbs Building of King's College

The Gibbs Building is said to be haunted by an eccentric fellow of the college, called Barrett, who had an apartment on *A* Staircase. Barret was a decidedly morbid person, who kept a coffin in his rooms.

As he grew old, Barrett was noticed to have an increasingly worried and frightened manner. He lost much of his money, and was dogged by bad luck. The reasons for this were not precisely understood, but it was rumoured that he was being haunted by dark forces.

One night mysterious screams were heard in Barrett's lodgings, and the next morning he was found dead in his coffin. It was widely rumoured that he had not been laid there by human agency, but by spiritual entities with which he had been communicating during his sinister life.

Every year, on the anniversary of Barrett's death, his screams reverberate along *A* Staircase, to alarm and terrify generations of students and staff.

King's College has an additional claim to fame for connoisseurs of supernatural literature, as it was the home of Montague Rhodes James (1862–1936), whom many people regard as the author of the best ghost stories in the English language.

Montague, who signed himself M R James, the name by which he is best known, entered King's College as a student in 1882. Graduating with first class honours in 1885, he became a Fellow, and later Master, of the college.

M R James's careers an author of supernatural fiction began in 1893, when he read a story he had written to The Chitchat Club, an informal University social organisation. The response was so enthusiastic that he was asked to write more, and his ghost stories became a feature of the University Christmas, when he entered the room, extinguished all the candles except one, and sat down to declaim his latest tale to the enthralled gathering.

In 1904 he published some of his most appreciated tales as *Ghost Stories Of An Antiquary*. This became one of the most influential works of its kind, creating the antiquarian ghost tale, in which a student – often from Cambridge University – embarks on research, only to find his studies drawing him inexorably into an encounter with supernatural powers. Carefully avoiding 'blood and guts' horror, M R James's stories convey an eerie sense of mystery, which is best brought out when read aloud, and which can often become more apparent with repeated reading.

M R James wrote several other volumes of ghost stories. These have remained among the most popular and imitated works of supernatural fiction. One of his tales, *Casting The Runes*, was made into a feature film in 1957 with the title *Night Of the Demon*, but no dramatisation has fully conveyed his wonderful mastery of atmosphere and the subdued horror that builds up in his stories.

LITTLE ST MARY'S LANE

This lane runs alongside Little St Mary's Church, a highly attractive and spacious fourteenth century building, which contains a memorial to Godfrey Washington, an English great-uncle of George Washington. The church is named Little St Mary's to distinguish it from the larger Great St Mary's church on the Market Place.

The churchyard faces the rather forbidding north face of Peterhouse (*see* Peterhouse), but Little St Mary's Lane contains a row of very attractive old buildings. One of these, whose location the University authorities have tried to keep secret, contains a haunted room, where three occupants sensed a presence. One person described it as a little girl, another thought it was an elderly woman, and a third believed it to be a young woman.

Peter Tranchell, the director of music studies at Gonville and Caius College once visited a resident of the house who was sick in a top floor bedroom. Going downstairs to the kitchen he heard a noise of rhythmic beating on a block of wood. Returning upstairs he asked the invalid why he was knocking on wood, to which the sick person replied: 'You can't catch me out like that! It was you!'

Knocking noises have accompanied the appearance of other ghosts in Cambridge. This particular manifestation does not seem to have developed into anything more dramatic, but it has made an impression on people living in the house.

MAGDALENE STREET

Enid Porter, the curator of the Cambridge Folk Museum, was involved in two ghost hunts in Magdalene Street. In 1967 two people working in an office in the street told her how they had seen the ghost of an elderly man in a nearby house. Strangers to Cambridge, they had moved there with their work, and knew nothing about any previous residents of the area. But their description of the figure coincided with a person who had lived in that building when it was a house, and committed suicide there in the 1950s.

Enid Porter helped to identify another ghost that may still linger in the area. In 1950, a former Cambridge student who had recently completed his National Service, and married, rented a room over a shop in Magdalene Street. In the evenings, they noticed a burning smell, which they described as 'sweet' not like a cigarette, and not like burning cloth'. They told Enid Porter that they would search for a fire, or source of heat, but found nothing.

Enid Porter made enquiries in the area. An elderly man who lived nearby in Northampton Street said that many years previously a lighterman who navigated barges along the River Cam had lodged in the same rooms, where he smoked opium which he bought at King's Lynn docks.

The opium-smoking spirit may continue to haunt Magdalene Street. When conducting the Cambridge Ghost Walk, we pause to tell these stories in Fisher Lane, a passage leading off Magdalene Street near the River Cam. On six occasions between July 1998 and September 1999 people on the walk have said that they have noticed a smell like a strong perfume, or a sweet substance being burned; some people have even compared it to opium. Alan Murdie himself smelt it at about 9.35pm on a windy Tuesday evening in July 1999.

MONTAGUE ROAD

One warm day in the summer of 1924 Geoffrey Wilson, a boy of ten, was playing in the garden of his grandparents' house at 25 Montague Road.

Suddenly he noticed a beautiful young woman, with a rather delicate and frail appearance, lying in a hammock in the summer house. She seemed quite natural, and Geoffrey paid little attention to her. When he returned to the house he described the woman. His family were startled, and told him that he had described Stella Wilson, his father's younger sister.

The family were reticent about giving further details, so it was not until several years later that Geoffrey, who had been a shy and timid child, discovered that his aunt Stella had died of tuberculosis earlier that summer. She had tried to treat her condition by going into the garden on warm days, spending much time in a hammock in the summer house.

Geoffrey Wilson regarded this an isolated episode in his life, for he had no great interest in the paranormal, and never saw a ghost again. He said: 'you could, I think, describe Stella's as a kindly ghost, as she made no effort to frighten a timid boy'.

NEW SQUARE

On the morning of 15 November 1857 Margaret Wheatcroft awoke from her sleep in her home in New Square to witness her soldier husband's death, even though he was over 2,000 miles away at the time.

Margaret, the woman who saw this dramatic ghost, was born Margaret Bicheno in Cambridge in 1830, the daughter of a local tradesman. In 1851 she married German Wheatcroft, an army officer, at St Martin's in the Fields Church in London.

In September 1857 German Wheatcroft left England with the Sixth Dragoon Guards for India, where the Indian mutiny, a rebellion against British rule, had broken out. He left Margaret to stay with her family in their house at 19 New Square.

The Sixth Dragoon Guards sailed through the Mediterranean Sea. When they stopped at Malta, German bought a dress for Margaret, which he posted back to her in Cambridge.

When Margaret went to sleep on the night of 14 November she knew that her husband would have been on campaign with his regiment, but she did not know exactly where in India he would be, or if he would be engaged in combat at any particular time. But early on the morning of 15 November she woke to see German standing over her bed. He was wearing his military uniform, staring at her with wide eyes and an appearance of great anxiety, his face pale and his hair dishevelled, clutching his hands over his chest. His mouth was contracted and trembling, as if he were trying to speak, but he was unable to make any noise. Margaret had sufficient time to realise that she was not dreaming, but fully awake. German stood before her for more than a minute, fully solid and tangible, before vanishing into thin air.

Margaret was convinced that German had just been killed in action. She was not to know why he had appeared before her.

Perhaps his last thoughts were of his wife, and had somehow connected with her. Perhaps German wanted Margaret to know of his death. Perhaps he wanted to see her for one last time. Perhaps Margaret had been given a final opportunity to see her husband. His lips were moving, so he might have wished to pass some message on to her, although if this was so, they were both cruelly disappointed, for he could not speak.

It is important to remember that there is a five-hour time difference between India and England. Thus, when it is midnight in Cambridge it is 7 pm in India. Since Margaret had seen her husband in the early hours of 15 November she was convinced that her husband had died on the afternoon or the evening of 14 November.

From 15 November Margaret began to wear the black dresses normally worn by Victorian widows when mourning for their husbands. A female friend, who was unaware of what had happened, invited Margaret to a fashionable concert, thinking this would provide her with an excellent opportunity to show off the dress German had sent from Malta. Margaret declined, saying it would be wrong to attend such an event so soon after her husband's death.

It took time for news of military casualties to pass through official channels to be relayed back to Britain. But in December it was announced that German Wheatcroft had died in action at the capture of Lucknow, one of the most important rebel strongholds.

Margaret Wheatcroft received a War Office Telegram:

We are to certify that it appears, by the records of this office, that Captain German Wheatcroft, of the 6 Dragoon Guards, was killed in action on 15 November 1857.

Margaret Wheatcroft was unhappy to receive this telegram, not just because it announced her husband's death, of which she was already aware, but because it said that German had died on 15 November. She had seen her husband standing above her on the morning of 15 November, when it would still have been 14 November in India. She was therefore certain that he had died on 14 November. She instructed her solicitor to ask the War Office to change their record of his date of death. The War Office refused, saying that the appearance of a ghost was an insufficient justification to alter an official despatch.

In March 1858 one of German Wheatcroft's fellow officers returned to England. This officer had served alongside German and asserted that German had been struck in the chest by a shell fragment when leading some troops in an attack on an outlying fortification before Lucknow, on the afternoon of 14 November. Carried off the battlefield, German remained conscious for some time, and tried to talk, but his wound prevented him from speaking. Dying several hours later, he was buried under a wooden cross with the inscription:

G.W., 14th of November 1857

Sir Colin Campbell, the commander of the British army at the siege of Lucknow, had drawn up a list of casualties after the rebel stronghold had been taken. In the confused aftermath of the siege he had listed all casualties as if they had died in the final assault on 15 November, without mentioning preliminary actions on previous days.

Not only had Margaret Wheatcroft seen her husband at the time of his death, but she had also seen him in the condition he would have been at the time, holding the place where he had been wounded.

Thus Margaret Wheatcroft was proved right. She had been

correct in assuming that her husband had died on 14 November, and the War Office had been incorrect when it sent her a telegram giving her husband's death as 15 November.

Shortly afterwards Margaret Wheatcroft required a duplicate copy of the telegram announcing her husband's death. When it arrived from the War Office she found that the date of death had been altered to 14 November.

Margaret Wheatcroft was later interviewed by representatives of the Society for Psychical Research, who regarded her experience as one of the most remarkable cases of a crisis apparition, where a person in great distress – often near death – is seen by another person a great distance away.

Margaret Wheatcroft's vision was even more remarkable for, at the height of British Imperial power, she caused the War Office, perhaps the most inflexible and dogmatic of all imperial institutions, to alter an official despatch.

NEWMARKET ROAD

Early in 1915, as Britain mobilised for the First World War, a company of nine military policemen was billeted in Newmarket Road, in a house on the Newmarket Road which had been unoccupied for seven years.

At midnight, the military policemen were simultaneously awakened by noises running around the house. These were followed by the materialisation of the shadowy outline of a man, which then vanished into thin air.

Finding courage in numbers, the military policemen searched the house from top to bottom, yet found nothing that could have created the noises, or made any optical illusions. Enquiring in the neighbourhood next morning, they were told that the house had stood empty because previous occupants had been frightened away by ghosts. On reporting the story, the local newspapers added that the policemen were strangers to the area, and knew nothing about the house when they moved in.

Military personnel continued to be billeted in the house, but no further activity was observed, prompting a newspaper reporter to suggest that 'the ghost has realised his duty to King and Country and has come to the conclusion that it would be an unpatriotic action further to interrupt the well-earned rest of hard-working soldiers'.

PETERHOUSE

Peterhouse, the oldest college in Cambridge University, was founded in 1284 by Hugh de Balsham, Bishop of Ely, and dedicated to St Peter. The college hall was built in 1286, and still stands on the south of the main courtyard: the earliest purpose-built college building in Cambridge.

The north face of Peterhouse, adjoining the churchyard of Little St Mary's Church, stands in an enclosed space, facing away from the sun and thus presents a dark, gloomy air. The passage running from Little St Mary's Lane to the college's north entrance has a strange atmosphere, and a Dean of Peterhouse once performed an exorcism to remove a dark presence from the corner of the quadrangle overlooking the churchyard.

Several people attending the Cambridge Ghost Walk have said that, as children at the start of the 1960s, they were warned away from the area. Others, such as an Italian woman who attended the Cambridge Ghost Walk with Ghost Club members in November 1998, say they feel uneasy in the passage leading to the north entrance.

In the mid-twentieth century a story circulated around the College

North face of Peterhouse

that a Blue Lady haunted *F* Staircase, which forms part of the college's original thirteenth century buildings. The Blue Lady was said to have been a Victorian woman who was associated with the college, although her identity was uncertain.

Over 1997 there were several ghost sightings in the Combination Room, a fifteenth-century chamber at the west end of the thirteenth-century Hall. The Hall and the Combination Room are connected through a passage in a fifteenth-century turret on the south. This turret, in which a bell was once hung, contains a spiral staircase.

At 9.30 pm on 17 April 1997 two college waiters, Paul Davies and Matthew Speller, descended the spiral staircase in the turret, to the Combination Room. As they entered, a white hooded figure materialised in the centre of the room, and glided to the oriel window in the south wall, where it disappeared. As the figure crossed the floor Paul Davies and Matthew Speller heard knocking sounds from the panelling, and rattling on the doors.

Badly shaken by their experience, they told the college Dean, Dr Graham Ward, a respected theologian.

Other members of the catering staff then began to report how they had noticed sudden temperature drops in the Combination Room, and heard knocking behind the panelling.

On 27 October, Dr Ward was hosting an official college function in the Hall. At 8.30 that evening Paul Davies entered the Combination Room. It was well lit, and two coal fires were blazing in the grates. Once again he was dumb-struck as the white figure materialised in the centre of the room. Paul Davies called Matthew Speller, and the college Butler, Mark Cooke, who rushed into the room to see the figure gliding to the oriel window as before. And, as before, they heard knocking on the walls and rattling on the doors. They rushed into the Hall to Dr Ward, who was sitting at high table, and told him that the ghost had appeared again.

It rather broke University protocol for the Dean to leave the Hall during an official function, but he was anxious to see the ghost. When he entered the Combination Room the ghost had vanished, but Dr Ward noticed that the room had become cold, despite two roaring coal fires. Dr Ward vouches for the integrity of Paul Davies, Matthew Speller and Mark Cooke, and for the look of stark terror on their faces after the sightings.

It was noted that both appearances occurred at the same time of day, allowing for the fact that the clocks had been moved back one hour for winter.

At the start of December, the college bursar, Andrew Murison, went into the Combination Room. Going to a fruit bowl to take some fruit he heard knocking on the walls, and sensed a cold, clammy presence behind him. He turned around and saw a small man wearing a jacket with a wide collar, and holding a large hat. He thought it was a member of the college staff, until he observed the figure's unusual clothes. In a few seconds the figure quietly disappeared in front of him. Dr Murison then noticed that the Combination Room had become very cold, although an open fire was burning in the grate.

The Combination Room ghost suddenly came to media attention on 19 December, when it was reported in the national press, on Radio Four, and even on the television news and Ceefax service. Most reporters suggested that the ghost was James Dawes, a fellow of Peterhouse who hanged himself on 27 September 1789. He left no message to explain why he wished to end his life, but this may have been because of his involvement in an election scandal, when he supported an unsuccessful attempt to place an unpopular person in charge of the college.

In 1786 Dr Edmund Law, the Master of Peterhouse, died. James Dawes favoured Daniel Longmire, another fellow of the college, to succeed Dr Law. Daniel Longmire was a friend of the Bishop of Ely, and the Bishop used technicalities in the college rules to impose Daniel Longmire as master on 27 September 1787.

Only James Dawes attended Daniel Longmire's inauguration ceremony. The other fellows contested the appointment in court. James Dawes objected to this, but was overruled. In court the judge decided that Daniel Longmire could not be Master. This was hardly James Dawes' fault, but Thomas Walker, the college historian, suggested that his involvement in the affair may have played on his mind and led to his suicide. The fact that James Dawes hanged himself on 27 September 1789, the anniversary of the day when Daniel Longmire became master, lends support to this theory.

James Dawes' obituary, in the *Gentleman's Magazine*, a London journal, said he hanged himself from the bell rope of the college chapel, and Thomas Walker accepted this statement. However, it would have been difficult for James Dawes to do this. The bell ropes are hung below the organ, in a space which is only ten feet high. If any weight is placed on the rope it automatically drops and rings the bell. Had James Dawes wished to hang himself on the chapel bell rope, he would have had to climb to the top of the chapel, and muffle or immobilise the bell. Even then, on tying himself to the bell ropes, he might only have fallen to the floor. And, although it is hard to understand the ways of a ghost, why would James Dawes haunt the Combination Room if he died in the College Chapel?

In 1999 the bill for James Dawes' coffin was discovered in the college archives. This said that he hanged himself from the bell rope in the fifteenth century turret which connects the Hall and the Combination Room.

The bill was drawn up by people who would have been present in Peterhouse at the time of James Dawes' death, and can be regarded as more accurate than the account in the *Gentleman's Magazine*. This also gives a plausible method of suicide, as it would have been easier for James Dawes to ascend to the top of the turret and muffle the bell. After tying himself to the bell rope he would have fallen a considerable distance. This would also explain why James Dawes' ghost would haunt the Combination Room.

These appearances, in the same room of Peterhouse, in a single year, witnessed by several reliable people, represent one of the most striking examples of a haunting in Britain in recent times.

The Peterhouse Turret where James Dawes hanged himself

THE HAUNTED PHOTOGRAPHIC STUDIO

Staff at the Cambridge Photographic Studio in St Botolph's Lane believe that the building is haunted. They have heard rumours that noises have been heard on the staircase and in upstairs rooms. Some assistants who served at the counter said that they noticed a man's feet going up the stairs, but that as soon as they caught sight of him, he vanished. Although the building which houses the studio is of some age, the ghost itself may not be very old, for it wore modern trousers and shoes.

THE PHANTOM PICTURE

Trumpington Street is the setting for the story of a phantom picture, which may be unique in the annals of psychical research, for the authors can find no episode like it in any other factual or fictional ghost story.

At the end of the nineteenth century a woman saw a house in Trumpington Street advertised for sale, and went to view it with the possible intention of purchase. A maid showed the woman into a ground floor sitting room and went to call the mistress.

Looking around the room, the woman saw the portrait of a lady hanging above the mantelpiece. The figure in the painting wore a bright green dress and a hat with a red feather, but the most alarming thing about it was the sinister and unpleasant expression on the sitter's face. When the proprietor of the house came downstairs the woman went into the drawing room to discuss the purchase. At the end of the conversation the owner said: 'I think perhaps I ought to tell you that there is a silly story about the house being haunted, but I don't suppose that will affect your decision'.

Intrigued by this, the woman asked if anybody had seen the ghost. The home owner replied that the ghost was supposed to take the form of a woman wearing a bright green dress and a hat with a red feather.

'Oh!' replied the woman, 'You mean the lady whose portrait hangs over the mantelpiece in the room I was first shown into.'

'Portrait?' replied the startled homeowner. 'There is no portrait in that room!'

The homeowner and the woman returned to the sitting room. Hanging above the mantelpiece was a country landscape. The woman had seen a ghost – not in the form of a living human, but in the form of an oil painting.

Pub Ghosts

Paranormal phenomena have been observed at four Cambridge hostelries – the Eagle, the Red Cow, the Pickerel and the Oyster Tavern.

The Eagle in Bene't Street has a long-standing reputation as a haunted building.

There is an oral tradition that two young boys who died in mysterious circumstances here appear in an upstairs window.

Two people attending the Cambridge Ghost Walk on separate occasions have told us about a girl who appears on the staircase at the Eagle. One of them said that in about 1959 she appeared in a glowing light, holding a lighted candle in a silver candlestick. The other person told us that a Victorian girl dressed in black appeared on the staircase in 1977.

Could some children have met with a tragedy or an experience that somehow impressed itself on the Eagle public house?

A ghost of a man who is only visible from the knees upwards is said to appear at the Red Cow in Corn Exchange Street. Over the years the floors inside the Red Cow have been altered, and the ghost is thought to walk along an earlier floor level. A person attending the Cambridge Ghost Walk told us that he was seen in January 1999.

The following March a lady in the bar of the Red Cow felt a hostile presence which so frightened her that she ran upstairs.

The Pickerel Inn in Magdalene Street lies alongside Fisher Lane, the haunt of an opium-smoking ghost (*see* Magdalene Street). Janis Spink, a manager of the Pickerel, said that a landlady is said to have thrown herself into the Cam, and her ghost is believed to haunt the Pickerel. Two staff members who once lived in the pub said the room they slept in always had a cold feel to it, and they woke up in the night to feel a strange 'presence' floating in the room around them.

Two landlords hanged themselves from the cellar hook, which is still in the pub.

At the end of 1979 ghosts were observed at the Oyster Tavern in Northampton Street. Noises were heard on the floors of upstairs rooms. An electric light in an upstairs room was persistently turned off, but it would always come on again. People outside the tavern often saw the light turn on through the window when the room was known to be empty.

Then, one midnight in January 1980, the manager's wife and a barmaid saw a figure with spiky hair and a high collar standing in the middle of the bar.

Since all the customers had left, they thought it was one of the staff. When they found all the personnel in another part of the building they were terrified to think that they had seen a ghost.

Three weeks later, in February, both women saw the figure in the bar again. As two women had seen the figure simultaneously, it could not have been dismissed as imagination. The barmaid was so frightened that she refused to go into the bar again after closing time.

The Oyster Tavern has since changed management, and is now called Michel's Brasserie. Psychic energy may have dispersed, for the present staff say that nothing has been seen or reported in recent years, although there were rumours that a presence could be sensed in the centre of the bar.

Sceptics may argue that indulgence in one kind of spirit increases the likelihood of seeing other kinds of spirits. However, it might be possible that the ambience in a public hostelry could make people more susceptible to psychic phenomena. An alternative explanation might be that a pub is a building where many people come to socialise, so that if any paranormal activity is observed in a pub, news of the event will circulate among pub-goers, and thus obtain a wide audience.

Some ghosts may have disturbed or frightened the people who saw them, but drinkers may receive an unexpected shock in the Eagle, for a table in the pub is said to tilt up at unexpected moments. Readers had best hold on tight to their glasses when they go to the Eagle, or they may find themselves upset by spirits in more ways than one!

RADIO CAMBRIDGESHIRE

Many of the paranormal phenomena described in this book have been witnessed in the older buildings in the city. But modern buildings can be haunted as well. The headquarters of Radio Cambridgeshire was opened in Hills Road in 1982. As an up-to-date broadcasting centre it must be one of the most modern buildings in the city, where a team of trained technicians is employed.

Yet many staff believe that one of the studios is haunted. The room is said to have a strange atmosphere, and a distinct presence can be sensed there. It may even be capable of some malevolence, for racks of tapes have been thrown across the studio. The studio becomes particularly sinister at night, when some disc jockeys refuse to broadcast from it, or even enter the room.

Whatever there may be in the building, it can obviously upset the staff, and even broadcasting equipment. Evidently, being modern does not exempt a building from sinister activity.

St John's College

St John's College has been the scene for phenomena which have been open to different interpretations.

St John's College

The ghost of Dr James Wood is said to appear on *O* Staircase of the second court of St John's College.

Wood was the son of a Lancashire weaver, who won a place at the college in 1778. He occupied a garret leading off *O* Staircase. Too poor to afford a fire, or even to buy candles to light his room, he studied on the staircase by the glow of the rush candle in the stairway passage and the light coming from under the wealthier undergraduates' doors, his feet wrapped in straw to protect them from the cold.

When Wood took his degree in 1782 he achieved the best results of any student that year, and became a fellow of St John's College. He later became Master of the College, and his books became the University's standard mathematical texts. On his death in 1839, when he was wealthy and respected, he left his large private fortune to his old college.

Yet the memory of his early days never left him, and his ghost can still be seen reading on the staircase where he worked as a poor student.

But in July 1998 a Mr Clark, a retired porter from the college, came on the Ghost Walk. He admitted that when going on his rounds in the early hours of the morning he would rattle a large key chain to give the impression that a ghost was haunting the college corridors!

More dramatic and controversial phenomena occurred near St John's College in 1694. This was documented by Abraham de la Pryme, who studied at St John's from 1690 to 1694, and later became a clergyman and historian.

When he was twelve, Abraham de la Pryme began to keep a diary, in which he recorded events that interested him, rather than his personal experiences. In May 1694, while on vacation from Cambridge, he received letters describing how a house opposite St John's College, occupied by Valentine Austin, a painter, was believed to be haunted.

When we try to understand the phenomena we have the disadvantage that Abraham de la Pryme was only reporting information at second-hand. Nevertheless, we can assume that it was supplied by College friends who were reasonably honest and intelligent, and who were writing while events were still fresh in their minds.

Activity lasted for about four weeks, being focused on the bedroom where Valentine Austin and his wife slept, described as 'a low ceiled room with a cellar under it'. From mid-April strange noises were heard around Valentine Austin's house. After a week these grew in intensity, and pebbles and stones were thrown through a hole under the door. This attracted spectators, and Valentine Austin and his wife allowed people to explore their house to search for the cause of the disturbances – apparently without success.

Events reached a climax during the fourth week, from two o'clock one Monday morning, when 'a great hollow noise was heard', accompanied by the ringing of metal. Windows were broken by small stones and the smell of brimstone was left hanging in the air.

By the next evening over sixty people had gathered outside St John's College in the hope of witnessing more phenomena. Ghost hunters probably disturbed the Austins more than any ghost, especially some students from St John's, who came into the house to look for ghosts, but then sent to a nearby ale-house for tobacco and pitchers of ale, and spent the rest of the night singing and joking in the house.

On Wednesday night the Reverend John Walker, the vicar of the Church of the Holy Sepulchre – better known as the Round Church – brought several people into the Austin's house to

The Round Church

pray. (Abraham de la Pryme does not specify if this was to stop the activity, or request further manifestations.)

As Walker and his colleagues prayed, a great bellowing noise was heard, and a paint pot hurtled through the window, shattering the glass, and narrowly missing Walker.

There were about 100 people outside the house, who were more frightened than the people inside. 'Away they all ran as if the Devil was in them' wrote Abraham de la Pryme. The

Reverend John Walker and his companions stayed to finish their prayers, then left in a hurry, although Walker used his experiences as the basis for his next two sermons at the Round Church.

The following Sunday night the Austins received some recompense for their inconvenience, as coins to a total value of six shillings were thrown into the room.

At the end of the rather dramatic fourth week four students of St John's College made a pact to go with pistols to Valentine Austin's house when activity was next reported, and fire them in direction from whence noise came. They seem to have been of the opinion that if the phenomena were being manufactured this might expose the person who was responsible, or frighten him away.

On Monday night, hearing that activity was starting, they rushed across the road and into the house with loaded pistols. But there were already several people in the room, who – not unreasonably – were quite alarmed by their entrance, and persuaded them not to fire their guns. The students eventually went away, but perhaps the crisis caused by four armed men bursting into the haunted room, ready to shoot, caused a counter-shock which cleared the air. Valentine Austin's house was no longer troubled by such phenomena as we have described.

The great Cambridge scientist, Isaac Newton, was passing the house one Monday night. He dismissed the activity as the work of 'mere cheats and impostures'.

Abraham de la Pryme also dismissed the affair as a fraud. Going back to Cambridge he asked about the phenomena, and found out that the information he had been sent was accurate. But most of his friends in Cambridge were as sceptical as he was.

We know nothing about Valentine Austin, except that he was a painter, and that he shared a house opposite St John's College with his wife. It is uncertain if any children, relatives, or other people shared the house with them; Abraham de la Pryme mentions none.

If the phenomena were fraudulent, Valentine Austin and his wife must have been manufacturing them themselves, or in collusion with others. If not, they may have been victims of a practical joker.

Why would the Austins create the fraud? To make money, or to attract attention, or just to play a joke with the people of Cambridge? Yet, apart from the instance when six shillings was thrown into the house, there is no evidence that they gained any financial profit or amusement. Instead, their privacy was invaded, their sleep was disrupted, and their windows were broken, and glass was more expensive in real terms in the seventeenth century than it is now.

The possibility that a practical joker was involved could be considered but, unfortunately, we cannot know if anybody had any animosity towards Valentine Austin, or if his house was in any way suitable for staging special effects.

Yet, although many people came to watch the activity, many of whom were openly sceptical, none of them seems to have been able to detect any trickery.

Had anybody been able to demonstrate that the activity was in any way fraudulent, or that anybody stood to gain from it, the sceptical Abraham de la Pryme would probably have mentioned this. Yet he does not.

The other possibility is that, for some reason which we cannot now understand, psychic forces were unleashed on the Austins. As with Simon Ockley at the Castle, it seems that they were tormented by a poltergeist, an invisible force which creates strange noises and causes objects to move (*see* Cambridge Castle).

The phenomena took one of the patterns familiar to poltergeist activity: noises, which grew in intensity, followed by the movement of objects – in this case showers of stones – and 'apports' – solid objects which apparently materialise in the air.

It is also interesting to notice that, although stones were thrown at the house, and windows were broken, nobody seems to have been physically hurt. In fact it seems strange that a paint pot could have been hurled through a window when people were in the house without striking anybody. This is another part of poltergeist phenomena: although people might be disturbed, or irritated by forces, poltergeists hardly ever cause physical harm, and objects thrown through the air almost always miss people.

It is a pity that we know nothing about the Austins. We cannot know if they were suffering from some stress or inconvenience in 1694. But it seems that they were the unwilling victims of a poltergeist attack, which eventually either spent itself, or else was dispelled by the impact of another psychological shock.

St Mark's Vicarage

The modern vicarage of St Mark's Church in Barton Road, Cambridge, is haunted by a forlorn young woman who appears to be a tidy spirit, but not above having the occasional smoke. Psychic activity in the vicarage has been independently attested to by three vicars in succession.

Canon Bill Loveless moved into St Mark's Vicarage in 1967 with his wife Betty. One night they were disturbed by persistent banging on their bedroom door, and crashing noises elsewhere in the house. Betty Loveless then saw the figure of a young girl standing in the bedroom. Canon Loveless continued to hear crashing sounds in the attic. But when he retired in 1987 he said nothing about his experiences to his successor, Canon Philip Spence, who arrived with his wife Monica. A few months later Canon Spence telephoned Canon Loveless to ask if he had noticed anything unusual about the vicarage. One night he had been arranging some bedroom furniture. There was a glass-topped dressing table in the bedroom. He had folded some lace doilies and put them in a drawer, and left the table's glass top standing on its side on the floor. The next morning the family woke to find the glass plate above the table, with the lace doilies underneath. Monica Spence said the ghost 'was always doing helpful things and we did not feel frightened at all'.

A stranger experience awaited Canon Christine Farringdon who arrived in March 1996, quite unaware of the previous vicars' experiences. She saw 'a forlorn young woman' standing at the window. But when she entered the house she found that it was empty, and when she went to the window where she had seen the forlorn young woman she found it was difficult to stand at the window. Since then Canon Farringdon has sometimes come into the empty house to notice the smell of tobacco smoke.

Neither vicar felt threatened by the ghostly activity. Betty Loveless thought the figure was a servant girl who was not at rest, and Canon Spence thought that she might have been keeping up her duties by tidying up after the family.

Canon Farringdon has noticed a feeling of somebody feeling a bit lost, but neither she nor anybody else had noticed any malevolence, and all three were able to talk of their experiences on *Signs and Wonders*, an Independent Television Programme shown on 30 November 1997, when they discussed their beliefs in an afterlife.

St Michael's Church

This fourteenth-century church served only a small parish in the town centre, which was united with Great St Mary's parish in 1908. St Michael's Church was hardly ever used for the next 58 years.

In 1963 two young men called Alan Attesley and Derek Cowling spent their weekends cleaning the dust and débris that had accumulated in the church during the long period of disuse.

One Saturday in summer, at about 11 am, they entered the church by the south door, under the tower, as they normally did.

St Michael's Church

They were walking up the aisle, when Alan Attesley saw a light gliding through the building – a ball of light, about thirty inches in diameter, giving off a luminescent blue-white glow, it moved from the south door, through which they had just entered, travelling a little faster than walking speed. The floating ball then passed into Derek Cowling's field of vision.

Both men stood transfixed, and Derek Cowling later said 'there was a chill which sent a shiver down the spine, and one's whole attention was held, grippingly'.

St Michael's Church was re-opened as a public hall in 1966. It is not known if any activity has taken place there recently. Alan Attesley and Derek Cowling saw something which made a great impression on them. Possibly it was a natural effect, (as the lights at Cutter Ferry Path may have been). But it is also possible that psychic forces were stored in the church over the long period of disuse, and have since dispersed.

SIDNEY STREET

Busick Harwood, who was Professor of Anatomy in Cambridge University from 1785 to 1814, lived at 15 Sidney Street, opposite Holy Trinity Church. His house was demolished in 1924, and the site is now occupied by Woolworth's.

It is possible that Busick Harwood dissected corpses in his Sidney Street house for, after his death in 1814, a human skeleton was unearthed in the garden.

Stories of Busick Harwood's experiments may have led to a belief that the house was haunted by a Black Lady. In 1820, when the house was bought by George Pryme, the first University Professor of Political Economy, servants refused to stay overnight for fear of the ghost. George Pryme and his family decided to show the servants that the Black Lady need not be feared by sleeping in the room she was supposed to haunt. This must have dispelled fears about the haunting, for the Black Lady troubled the house no more.

Entrance to 15 Sidney Street

SIDNEY SUSSEX COLLEGE

The most famous person to have studied at Sidney Sussex College was Oliver Cromwell, so perhaps it is appropriate that Oliver Cromwell's head should have been placed in the college chapel in 1960.

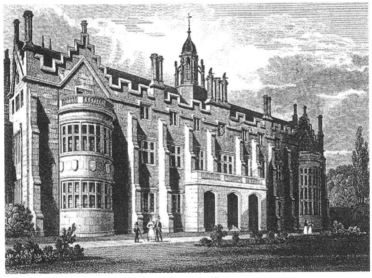

Sidney Sussex College

Oliver Cromwell was born in 1599, and entered Sidney Sussex in 1616, but did not complete his degree. This may have been because of his father's death, although it was not uncommon at the time for young gentlemen to spend a short period at a university to develop social and academic skills without actually taking a degree.

Although Cromwell spent much time at Cambridge in his later years, there is no record that he revisited Sidney Sussex, nor any record of any feelings that he may have held about the institution.

Cromwell died in 1658. His head has a long and strange

history that ends with its being laid to rest in Sidney Sussex College. After his death in 1658, his body was subjected to a post-mortem examination in which the top of his skull was cut open and his brain examined, while death masks were cast from his face. He was then buried in Westminster Abbey.

In 1660 Charles II returned to England as king. Before his arrival he pronounced an amnesty exonerating all participants in the Civil War for their actions, with the specific exception of those people who had participated in the execution of his father, King Charles I. It was too late to exact any punishment on Oliver Cromwell but, as a gesture of retribution, Cromwell's body was exhumed and, on 30 January 1661, the twelfth anniversary of Charles I's execution, it was publicly hanged at Tyburn, where the largest gallows in London stood. The site is now occupied by Marble Arch.

That evening, Cromwell's corpse was beheaded, which must have been a difficult process, as it took eight blows of an axe to cut the neck. Long-standing custom held that the heads of people executed for crimes against the state were displayed in London: often on the city gates. Oliver Cromwell's head was displayed on a wooden stake above the Houses of Parliament.

It is uncertain what happened to the rest of Cromwell's body. It has been suggested that the body was buried under the gallows at Tyburn. Other traditions say that a few sympathisers buried it in a secret location. A vault at Newburgh Priory in Yorkshire

Oliver Cromwell

80

is suggested as his burial place, but this is not open to examination.

Cromwell's head remained on display above the Houses of Parliament until November 1688, when it was blown down during a storm. A sentry on guard duty, often named as Private Barnes, picked it up and took it home with him. The government and the commanding officers of the army threatened severe punishment on the person who had taken it, which seems strange, for they had displayed little love for Cromwell's memory, and had conspicuously failed to show his remains any honour.

Private Barnes was therefore in the unenviable position of possessing a decapitated head, which can have been of little use or ornament, but which he dared not dispose of, for fear of incurring the wrath of the government. He is believed to have hidden the head in the chimney of his house, where he kept it secret until he lay on his death bed in 1702, when he told a few relatives about it.

Perhaps official wrath had abated by then, for the head became a useful legacy to his wife's family, who sold it to Claudius du Puy, a Swiss cloth merchant who ran a private museum in London. This museum was dispersed on du Puy's death, and by 1773 Oliver Cromwell's head had come into the possession of an actor called Samuel Russell, a distant descendant of Oliver Cromwell's daughter, Frances. Samuel Russell offered to sell the head to the Master of Sidney Sussex College, who turned his offer down. Russell therefore exhibited the head in Long Acre, near Covent Garden in London.

In 1787 the head was bought by James Cox, a London antique dealer and showman, for £118. He must have regarded it as a desirable purchase, for this was more than a year's wages for most people at the time, but it still represented a profitable investment, for in 1799 James Cox re-sold it for £230 to three brothers called Hughes, who placed it on display in Old Bond

Street. An advertisement in the Morning Chronicle of 18 March 1799 read:

> The real embalmed head of the powerful and renowned usurper, Oliver Cromwell, is now exhibited at Mead Court, Old Bond Street (where the rattlesnake was shown last year). Tickets half a crown.

Oliver Cromwell had been reduced to sharing the stage with a rattlesnake. Half a crown seems rather a large sum for the time, so perhaps it is not surprising that the exhibition failed. The head then passed into the possession of John Cranch, a historian from Devon who had helped to organise the exhibition.

In 1814 the head was purchased by Dr Josiah Wilkinson, whose descendants retained possession. In 1932 the Wilkinson family loaned the head to the faculty of medicine at London University for examination. Executed criminals' heads had been publicly exhibited in many British and Continental European Countries over past centuries, so there was a realistic possibility that the head need not have been that of Oliver Cromwell. But its measurements were found to correspond with those of Oliver Cromwell's death masks. It also showed the prominent wart over the right eye which had prompted Oliver Cromwell's proverbial instruction to artists that his portraits should not be flattering, but should show him 'warts and all'. Surviving facial hair was found to match the colour of the hair on these portraits. It was discovered that the head had been embalmed, and that there were marks of axe-blows on the neck.

The master of the armouries at the Tower of London examined the spike on which the head was transfixed, and found that it was a seventeenth-century pikestaff. He also noticed a wormhole penetrating both the head and the staff, which showed that the two had been aligned together for a lengthy period. It was agreed that no other decapitated head could show so many characteristics by pure chance.

Twenty-eight years later, the Wilkinson family decided that Oliver Cromwell's last documented remains should finally be laid to rest in Sidney Sussex College.

On 25 March 1960 the college chaplain conducted a ceremony in which the head was interred in the college chapel. The service was attended by the Master of the College and three Fellows, together with Dr Wilkinson and his sister. In view of the possibility that supporters of the monarchy, or those who resented Oliver Cromwell's memory, might try to desecrate the skull, its exact location in the chapel remains a secret, known only to a few college officials.

Sidney Sussex was a focus of paranormal activity before this macabre memento of its most famous student was placed there. In 1841 a particularly terrifying ghost was seen in the Master's Lodge, which occupied the upper floors of the central block of the Hall Court. On Friday 6 August, 'at about the dread hour of midnight', the nursery maids in the Master's Lodge were going to bed after many tiring hours of work, when they heard strange and mysterious noises move around the top floor, and then heading down the stairs.

The noise then ceased, leaving a quiet and stillness more ominous than any sound. For a few moments the maids were unaware of further activity. Then the bedroom door slowly opened, and an apparition slowly materialised before the horror-struck maids. The dim outline of a human figure, it resembled a shadow, but with more substantial form and capable of unaided movement. It had a ghostly white head on a small torso with no arms, and walked slowly on two white legs.

Petrified with fear, the maids eventually recovered their powers of movement. Running around the shadowy apparition they fled shrieking through the door and down the stairs.

The master's family and the whole household were awakened by the terrified maids' panic, and everybody in the house had soon heard their story. It was suspected that they were the victims of a practical joker, but all the doors and windows in the house were found to be locked from the inside, and all the occupants had convincing proof that they had been in bed.

When the maids' room was searched nobody could be found hidden, and there were no physical traces of any unwanted intruder, but a distinct and unusual perfume permeated the air. Constables from the borough's newly-established police force were called, who testified to the strange smell, and the affair was considered sufficiently serious for two of the borough magistrates to be asked to come to the lodge to investigate, although they do not seem to have discovered anything.

The story helped to fuel a circulation war between the local newspapers. *The Cambridge Advertiser*, a comparatively new local publication, described the event in detail, and its report was copied verbatim by no less an authority than *The Times*.

The more traditional *Cambridge Chronicle* considered it beneath its dignity to report the story – this makes one wonder if other ghosts were seen in Georgian or Victorian Cambridge and not reported by the newspapers.

Yet the story was too well attested to be dismissed as a practical joke or a hoax.

On 1 November 1967, just after Hallowe'en, Sidney Sussex was the setting for another mysterious event. That day an undergraduate called John Emslie went to visit his friend Peter Knox-Shaw, who lodged in a room leading off *H* Staircase on the south wing of Chapel Court. Finding Knox-Shaw's room empty, John Emslie decided to wait there for his friend's return.

Within a few minutes he began to feel a presence in the room. As he looked around he saw a shape forming in the air before him. He was then overcome with a horrible sensation of coldness flowing through him. His neck became stiff, and he even found it difficult to breathe. A presence then began to materialise in the form of a large mouth, suspended in mid-air, which slowly coagulated, turning into what he would later describe as 'the most terrifying spectacle of my life': a pale yellow emaciated head, floating in mid-air.

Eventually John Emslie overcame the petrifying sensation that was immobilising his body, and preventing him from breathing, to turn and flee from the room in stark terror, gasping for air as he fought the creeping paralysis from his face and throat.

Soon afterwards Peter Knox-Shaw returned to his college room on *H* Staircase, not knowing that his friend had sought to visit him, and certainly not suspecting that anybody could undergo such a horrifying experience in the room when for no reason which he could understand he felt cold and frightened. He then noticed the strong and putrid smell of rotting flesh mysteriously pervading the room. Later John Emslie returned to tell Peter Knox-Shaw of his earlier experience. The two undergraduates, by now thoroughly alarmed, began to discuss and compare their impressions of what had happened. Both third-year undergraduates, they were acquainted with University life, and with student pranks and hoaxes, but neither of them had seen, or even heard of, anything like this before. They became increasingly frightened, and eventually fled the room in panic, not to return again that night.

Another student, Michael Howarth, lived in the room above on *H* Staircase. He was engaged to Linda Nield-Siddall, a Newnham undergraduate. Unaware of the startling events that had taken place so close at hand, she was spending the following afternoon dozing on the bed in her fiancé's room when she noticed a large purple eye floating in mid-air before her bedroom door. At first she thought it to be an unusual trick of the light, but she then stood up and walked around the room, expecting that a change of vision or light would make the apparition vanish. Instead it stayed, disappearing and re-appearing in mid-air for ten minutes. Linda Nield-Siddall was not greatly frightened, but was rather unnerved, and eventually left the room.

In the following few days the eye was seen again by other students, and several people commented on feeling unusually cold and smelling something which was described as 'musty', 'earthy', 'like Oxo', or 'like Spam'. *Varsity* the University newspaper, commented that 'one amazing thing is that everybody takes it absolutely seriously'.

Knowledge of the phenomena spread, and other people, including psychic researchers, descended on Sidney Sussex College, but the increased number of visitors to *H* Staircase, and the passing of time, seem to have dispersed the activity.

As far as the authors know, the 1841 sighting had completely passed from memory; they re-discovered it when researching this book. Yet the 1841 and 1967 apparitions were similar in several ways: distorted parts of a human body materialising in mid-air, then disappearing, leaving a distinctly pungent odour which drew strong comments from those who smelt it. Possibly there are certain forces, as yet unknown, which can reappear in the same location over periods of time. Although both apparitions were treated with scepticism by some people who heard about them, those who met the witnesses were convinced of their sincerity. Neither sighting can easily be dismissed as a practical joke or hoax, and they have never been satisfactorily explained in rational terms.

Silver Street

On the evening of 21 November 1954 a student saw a ghost in Silver Street.

Returning from a visit to Oxford one evening, the student was walking westward down Silver Street, towards Queens' College.

At that date Queens', like most colleges, operated a curfew. It closed overnight, and students who were locked out after curfew could be disciplined and fined. Nearly all students broke curfew at some time, and would try to re-enter college by some devious method so as to avoid punishment. This student was planning to wait until Silver Street was empty, and then climb over the college wall.

As the student got within view of the Anchor pub he clearly saw an old man walking along the road in front of him. The

Queens' College

moon was not visible, but it was a clear night, and the main street light, fifty yards away, was lit. Thus he could clearly see that the old man had long, thinning silvery hair, was wearing a morning coat, and was walking with a stooped posture, holding his hands clasped behind his back. The student followed the old man for at least a minute and, being a faster walker, came increasingly closer.

At the time his main concern was how to climb over the college wall without being noticed. But as the student came within two paces of the old man's back, the old man simply disappeared. An old man had just vanished into thin air, a few feet in front of the student, on a clear November night! Although surprised by what he had seen (or not seen), the student scaled the college wall and ran to his rooms without being noticed by the staff.

He had no previous interest in psychical research, and had been sceptical on the subject, but as soon as he had closed the door behind him he sat down in his rooms and wrote a detailed account of his experience, which he presented to the Society for Psychical Research.

Since he was in breach of college regulations when he saw the ghost the student requested anonymity, but Frederick Stratton, the University Professor of Astrophysics, who was president of the Society for Psychical Research at the time, met the student to discuss his experience, and was convinced of his sincerity.

THE TOURIST INFORMATION OFFICE

The building in Wheeler Street which houses the Tourist Information Office housed the Cambridge Central Library from 1862, when it was built, until 1975, when a new library was opened in the Lion Yard.

John Pink, the first borough librarian, ran the library until 1905. Perhaps he became so attached to the building that he was unable to leave it for, when the caretakers heard the floors creaking at night, they believed it was John Pink still carrying out his rounds.

When Alan Murdie was speaking about ghosts on BBC Radio Cambridgeshire in 1998 a former employee of the library service telephoned to say that they had seen John Pink's ghost in the building in 1992. In August 1998 a tourist information worker told Alan Murdie that footsteps had been heard in the office. This person also said that shortly after the tourist information office opened, the building would be locked for the night, but when the staff came to work the next morning objects had been inexplicably moved.

Michael Petty, the former local studies librarian, was asked for a comment, and he confirmed that staff were aware of the story for as long as the building had been used as a library, and that the head caretaker had been convinced that John Pink was responsible for continued nocturnal clicking and creaking.

TRINITY COLLEGE

Trinity College has played an important role in psychical research. It is the original home of The Ghost Club, the oldest English organisation dedicated to the study of psychical phenomena, formed in 1851 by two members of Trinity College, Fenton Hort and Brooke Westcott. The prospectus, drawn up by Fenton Hort, described it as 'a society for the investigation of ghosts and all supernatural appearances and apparitions'.

The Ghost Club was perhaps the first organisation to be formed in the British Isles with the avowed aim of making a scientific and dispassionate study of the paranormal. Some of the more prominent members of the university joined, and 750 copies of Fenton Hort's prospectus gained a wide circulation.

Although the society did collect a number of stories and cases, it declined after some years, although some of the members went on to higher things. Fenton Hort became University Professor of

Neville's Court – Trinity College

Divinity, while Brooke Westcott became Bishop of Durham. Another member, Edward Benson, became Archbishop of Canterbury.

The Ghost Club was launched in London in 1862, revived in 1882, reorganised again by Harry Price in 1938, and continues to research ghostly sightings in Great Britain.

The college also has important associations with psychical research through three of its graduates: Henry Sidgwick, Frederic Myers and Edmund Gurney, who entered the college in 1855, 1860 and 1866 respectively. All three enjoyed outstanding careers and became Fellows of Trinity. Henry Sidgwick was an active member of the original Ghost Club, and this may have helped inspire him to form another association for the study of the paranormal in 1874. One of the people who joined was Eleanor Balfour, who played a leading role in starting the women's college at Newnham. Eleanor Balfour and Henry Sidgwick married in 1876.

Frederick Myers, Edmund Gurney, and Henry and Eleanor Sidgwick played a leading role in setting up the Society for Psychical Research in 1882. This was founded with the aim of studying supernatural phenomena scientifically, and turning psychical research into a respectable study. Early members of the Society for Psychical Research included William Gladstone, the Prime Minister, and Alfred, Lord Tennyson, the poet. Henry Sidgwick was chosen to be the Society's first president, while Frederick Myers and Edmund Gurney were secretaries.

In 1886 Edmund Gurney produced *Phantasms Of The Living* for the Society of Psychical Research: a study of over 700 so-called 'crisis apparitions', when a person sees another person who is a great distance away, usually when one of them is dying, or in need of urgent assistance (*see* New Square).

Between 1889 and 1894 Eleanor Sidgwick organised the Society's *Census Of Hallucinations*, in which 17,000 people were asked if they had seen or perceived a person or object which had no physical reality. It was found that one in ten of those questioned had done so.

Both books were written in a ponderous manner, and can make difficult reading, but these were the first efforts to make a statistical analysis of the supernatural, and they proved that at least one person in ten undergoes some form of psychic experience during their lifetime.

The Society for Psychical Research still functions, and is now one of the world's most respected institutions of its kind.

As a tribute to Henry Sidgwick, Frederic Myers and Edmund Gurney, the Perrott – Warwick studentship in psychical research was set up at Trinity College in 1940, the first academic post in psychical research at a British University.

The authors have heard two vague oral traditions that two figures in Victorian dress walk across the lawn at Trinity College.

William Howitt, a Victorian author who was greatly interested in spiritualism, published a *History Of The Supernatural* in 1863, which contains case studies which he believed proved the existence of an afterlife. These include a story that was told to William Howitt by the poet William Wordsworth, who was a personal friend. William Wordsworth's brother, Dr Christopher Wordsworth, was Master of Trinity College from 1820 to 1841. Christopher Wordsworth told William how a young student once arrived at Trinity College, and asked for lodgings. Dr Wordsworth obligingly directed the student to rooms which had just been vacated. A few days later the student asked to be moved elsewhere, because when he went to bed he locked the door from the inside, but every night he was awakened by the ghost of a child who wandered round the room, moaning, with the palms of its hands turned outward. Dr Wordsworth then told the student that this ghost had frightened the last occupant away, and other residents had complained about ghosts there. He had suspected that this might just have been a story that circulated, until people began to anticipate ghostly phenomena whenever they entered the room. And so when a stranger, with no knowledge of Cambridge, asked to stay at Trinity College, Dr Wordsworth could not resist the temptation to install him in the haunted room to find out if he would see the ghost. And this person, with no previous knowledge of the story, had seen the ghost, and had been frightened by his experience.

Perhaps Dr Wordsworth's experiment was unpleasant, but both he and William Wordsworth thought it proved that ghosts did exist.

In view of Trinity College's associations with paranormal research, perhaps it is appropriate that the college should have been the setting for a ghost sighting which led to the development of an important theory on the nature of hauntings.

Thomas Charles Lethbridge, better known as T C Lethbridge, studied archaeology at Trinity College from 1920 to 1923, but later turned to paranormal research (*see* Archaeology Museum).

T C Lethbridge said he experienced his first memorable psychic experience in Trinity College New Court. Late one night in 1922 he was sitting in the room of a fellow student (whom he identified as GW), facing the west side of New Court, overlooking the River Cam. As it neared midnight Lethbridge got up to leave, the door opened and a man entered, wearing a top hat and a hunting outfit. The figure walked a few paces forward, and rested his hands on a table in the centre of the room. Thinking it was a college porter, Lethbridge bade him 'good evening', and left, noticing that GW returned the statement, but that the mystery entrant did not reply.

Next morning Lethbridge met GW in Sidney Street, and enquired about the visitor. The irritated GW replied that nobody else had entered the room. They began arguing about this mysterious person. In exasperation, Lethbridge tried to describe the entrant, at which point he realised that the figure had a very strange appearance. He was small and slightly built, with an elongated, pointed face. Lethbridge then remembered that college porters were only obliged to wear top hats on Sundays, and this had been a week day, besides which no member of the college would normally wear a hunting costume – unless he was going hunting, which was unlikely at midnight!

Suddenly Lethbridge was struck by a startling realisation: the person's dress and appearance had been most unusual, his behaviour had not been quite normal, and GW had failed even to notice him enter the room. He realised that he must have seen a ghost! As the now amazed Lethbridge recollected his experience, he remembered that the figure had appeared in black, white and grey, and had walked without making any sound, as if a black-and-white cinema film was being projected into the room. This led him to form the theory, which has been studied by later paranormal researchers, that ghosts may be emotional 'photographs' caused by a person undergoing an emotional experience which somehow imprints itself on the scene where it occurs.

Lethbridge also suggested that, as time passes, the impression becomes fainter, and eventually disperses, as if the development of a photograph were being reversed, much as a picture may fade under a strong light.

Noticing that he had seen the ghost in a room near the River Cam, Lethbridge was among the first psychic researchers to suggest that ghosts often appear in damp areas, and that psychic manifestations might therefore be carried through water vapour, or even be forms of water vapour.

CONCLUSION

So ends our selection of ghost stories associated with the city of Cambridge. Some of these have been told us by people attending the Cambridge Ghost Walk, who often say that they do not normally disclose their experiences for fear of being laughed at or thought odd.

Almost every week we receive details of a new story or experience, and this suggests to us that ghostly and paranormal experiences are much more common among the population than is generally appreciated, even by ghost investigators.

In describing some examples of the paranormal phenomena that may be encountered in one small part of England, we hope that our book will help the reader who wishes to gain an understanding of ghosts or hauntings. Research in other parts of England will probably yield a similar crop of material.

If any readers have seen a ghost or undergone a psychic experience, they will now know that they are not alone.

References

Information on Cambridge ghosts, and many other aspects of Cambridge's long and interesting history, can be consulted in *The Cambridgeshire Collection*, the local studies department of the Cambridge Central Library.

Another very important source of information has been the files of the Society for Psychical Research, which are now kept at Cambridge University Library.

For information on graduates of Cambridge University, a good starting point is John Venn's *Alumni Cantabrigiensis* (1922–1927), a list of all those who studied at the University.

Another source of information on some individuals is the *Dictionary of National Biography*, which started publication in 1885, and is available in most libraries.

The Abbey House
Archives of the Society for Psychical Research case file H157.
(Dossier of statements collected by Frederick Stratton).
Alan Gauld 'The haunting of Abbey House, Cambridge'
Journal of the Society for Psychical Research
40 (1972) pp109–23. (Extracts from file H157).
Enid Porter *Cambridgeshire Customs and Folklore* (1969).
Arthur Beales Gray *Cambridge Revisited* (1921).
For Jacob Butler see an anonymous pamphlet *The History of Barnwell Abbey Near Cambridge With The Origin of Stourbridge Fair* (1806) and Charles Henry Cooper's *Annals of Cambridge* (1852–1908).

The Archaeology Museum
TC Lethbridge *Ghost and Ghoul* (1962).

The Haunted Bookshop
Cambridge Weekly News 20 August 1987.
The Cambridge Insider 22 January–4 February 1998.

Cambridge Castle
Simon Ockley's account is kept in the British Library at Lansdowne MSS 846. This was published in HO Evennett 'An ancient Cambridge poltergeist' *British Journal of Psychical Research* 2 (1929) pp172–179.

Christ's College
Arthur Ponsford Baker *A College Mystery* (1918).

CORPUS CHRISTI COLLEGE
Robert Masters *History of the College of Corpus Christi* (1753)
'Table Talk' column *Cambridge Daily News* 24 December 1904.
'A college ghost', *The Occult Review*, March 1905 pp129–133;
(written anonymously, but probably by Llewellyn Powys).
Arthur Beales Gray *Cambridge Revisited* (1921).
Shane Leslie *The Cantab* (1926) and T*he Film of Memory* (1938).
Patrick Bury *The College of Corpus Christi, A History From 1822 To 1952*
(1952).
C Pollock 'The story of the Corpus Ghost'
Corpus Association Newsletter 39 (1960) 14–15.
CHE Smyth 'The Corpus Ghost' 45 (1966) pp40–44.
Graham Chainey *A Literary History of Cambridge* (1985).
Archives of the Society for Psychical Research, case file H70.
Parish registers of St Benet's church, (kept at the Cambridgeshire Record
Office).

Cromwell Lodge
Archives of the Society For Psychical Research, case file G266.
Untitled paper, *Journal of the Society for Psychical Research* 10 (1901),
43–47.

Cutter Ferry Path
Cambridge Chronicle 25 January 1928.
Cambridge Independent Press 27 January 1928.
Cambridge Daily News 30 January 1928.
For the geography of this ghost sighting see the 1926
Ordnance Survey Map, 25 miles to the inch,
Cambridgeshire sheet XL14

Emmanuel College
Archives of the Society For Psychical Research, file H69.

The Folk Museum
Arthur Beales Gray Cambridge Revisited (1921), and information supplied by
the museum staff.

The Gogmagog Hills
Wendy Clark, Once Around Wandlebury (1985).
Arthur Gray 'On the Wandlebury Legend' Proceedings of the Cambridge
Antiquarian Society 15 (1910) pp53–62.
Glenys Goetinck 'The Wandlebury legend and Welsh romance'
Proceedings of the Cambridge Antiquarian Society
77 (1988) pp105–8.

PH Reaney The Place Names of Cambridgeshire and the Isle of Ely (1948). On the significance of Wandil see Jacqueline Simpson 'Waendel and the Long Man of Wilmington' Folklore 90 (1979) pp25–8.

Jesus College

Arthur Gray *A History of Jesus College*, Cambridge (1902), revised by Frederick Brittain (1979).
Arthur Gray *Brief Tedious Tales of Grantya and Gramarye* (1919)
Enid Porter *Cambridgeshire Customs And Folklore* (1969).
Cambridge Evening News 18 October 1977; 31 November 1977.
The Ghost Club Archives, 1882–1936, are kept in the British Library at Additional Manuscripts 52258–52273.

King Street

Cambridge Daily News 30 December 1959.

King's College

The ghost of the Gibbs building is described in M R James *Eton and Kings* (1929) and Shane Leslie *The Film of Memory* (1938).
M R James wrote four collections of ghost stories: *Ghost Stories of an Antiquary* (1904); *More Ghost Stories* (1911); *A Thin Ghost* (1919); and *A Warning to the Curious* (1925).
All these were incorporated into MR James *Collected Ghost Stories* (1931).
Some additional stories and supernatural writings appear in MR James *Casting The Runes And Other Stories*, edited by Michael Cox, (1982).
Ghosts And Scholars (1987) edited by Richard Dalby and Rosemary Pardoe, contains a selection of ghost stories in the Jamesian tradition, some set in Cambridge.

Little St. Mary's Lane

Cambridge Evening News 7 April 1971.

Magdalene Street

Cambridge Daily News 30 December 1959.
Enid Porter *Cambridgeshire Customs and Folklore* (1969).
Cambridge Evening News 27 August 1998.

Montague Road

Dennis Bardens *Ghosts and Hauntings* (1965).

Newmarket Road

Cambridge Daily News 16 January 1915.

New Square
Robert Dale Owen *Footfalls on the Boundary of Another World* (1860).
JH Ingram *The Haunted Houses and Family Traditions of Great Britain* (1884).
Edmund Gurney *Phantasms of the Living* (1886). (The Wheatcroft case does not appear in the 1918 re-publication of *Phantasms of the Living*.)
Jean Nelson and Eileen Webster *Bicheno, A Family From Over, Cambridgeshire* (1992–4). (Locates Margaret Wheatcroft's residence in New Square.)

Peterhouse
Cambridge Evening News 19 December 1997;
Times Higher Education Supplement 19 December 1997; 2 January 1998;
The Independent 20 December 1997;
Daily Mail 19 December 1997;
Daily Telegraph 19 December 1997;
The Times 19 December 1997;
Philip Pattenden 'What the butler saw: high spirits in college' *Peterhouse Annual Record* 1997–8, pp66–72.
For James Dawes *see* Thomas Alfred Walker *Admissions to Peterhouse ... A biographical register ... 1615–1911* (1912);
The Gentleman's Magazine October 1789; and
DA Winstanley *Unreformed Cambridge* (1935).

The Phantom Picture
Thomas Thornely 'The lady of Trumpington Street' *The Cam* February 1937, p62.

Pub Ghosts
Cambridge Evening News 9 February 1980.
Cambridge Evening News 27 August 1998.

St John's College
Cambridge Daily News 30 December 1959.
Enid Porter *Cambridgeshire Customs and Folklore* (1969).
The Diary of Abraham de la Pryme Surtees Society Publications, 54, 1870).

St Mark's Vicarage
Cambridge Evening News 27 November 1997.
Sunday Telegraph 30 November 1997.
Church Times 5 December 1997.

St Michael's Church
Archives of the Society for Psychical Research, case file H474.

Sidney Street
George Pryme *Autobiographical Recollections* (1870).

Sidney Sussex College
Karl Pearson and GM Morant *The Portraiture of Oliver Cromwell With Specific Reference To The Wilkinson Head* (1935).
C Parish 'The posthumous history of Oliver Cromwell's head', in *Sidney Sussex College, Historical Essays In Commemoration Of The Quatercentenary* edited by D Beales and H Nesbet (1996).
Nicholas Rogers and Christopher Parish *Cromwell and Sidney Sussex* – a pamphlet published by Sidney Sussex College, 1999
Cambridge Advertiser 11–18 August 1841.
Cambridge Chronicle 14 August 1841.
The Times 12 August 1841.
Varsity 18 November 1967.
Untitled account of activity *Sidney Sussex College Annual* 1989 p35.

Silver Street
Alan Gauld 'A Cambridge Apparition' *Journal Of The Society For Psychical Research* 38 (1955), pp89–91

The Tourist Information Office
Cambridge Evening News 4 October 1968.

Trinity College
Notes and Queries first series 9 (18 February 1854) pp150–1.
Life and Letters of Fenton John Anthony Hort by his son AF Hort (1896).
Life and Letters of Brooke Foss Westcott by his son A Westcott (1903).
Alan Gauld *The Founders of Psychical Research* (1968).
Renee Haynes *The Society for Psychical Research, 1882–1987, A History* (1982).
William Howitt *History of the Supernatural* (1863).
TC Lethbridge *Ghost and Ghoul* (1962).
The Ghost Club Archives 1882–1936 are kept in the British Library at Additional Manuscripts 52258–52273.